Mastering Character Design

This book is a comprehensive guide for artists looking to master character design, no matter their chosen style. It offers practical insights into the core principles used in animated projects, helping you understand how to accurately draw and construct shapes, as well as the key elements of design. The content covers not only human anatomy but also extends to animal forms, offering strategies to depict both with precision and with expression.

You'll learn how to draw essential features like eyes, lips, hands, and legs – both for humans and animals – while also delving into the way shapes convey musculature from various perspectives. The book emphasizes the importance of shape and size variation and how to achieve a strong, clear silhouette.

Above all, this book teaches you how to draw with intent and purpose. It focuses on making thoughtful decisions about each line to ensure clarity and informativity, while also guiding you in creating designs that are dynamic and full of life. With these skills, you'll be able to design characters with intention and draw them in a way that feels both effective and engaging.

Caroline Hu has been in the animation and creative business for way too long, specializing in character design and storyboarding, having worked at various studios, such as Warner Bros. and Disney. At night, she is an animation professor, a martial artist, and a parent. She lives in California with her family, her two smokin' hot rods and one that's non-smokin'.

Mastering Character Design

Design with Intent and Purpose

Caroline Hu

CRC Press
Taylor & Francis Group
Boca Raton London New York

CRC Press is an imprint of the
Taylor & Francis Group, an **informa** business

Designed cover image: Caroline Hu

First edition published 2026
by CRC Press
2385 NW Executive Center Drive, Suite 320, Boca Raton FL 33431

and by CRC Press
4 Park Square, Milton Park, Abingdon, Oxon, OX14 4RN

CRC Press is an imprint of Taylor & Francis Group, LLC

© 2026 Caroline Hu

ISBN: 9781032985053 (hbk)
ISBN: 9781032985039 (pbk)
ISBN: 9781003599005 (ebk)

DOI: 10.1201/9781003599005

Typeset in Utopia Std
by codeMantra

To KCH and all our four-
legged pals

Table of Contents

Foreword

Designing and drawing … it all starts with an inspiration, doesn't it? For me, it all started at a young age, watching *Scooby Doo* on a tiny television and knowing from that moment on, that that was what I wanted to do. Since then, I have found inspiration from other fellow designers, my favorites being Jean Gillmore, Stephen Silver, Nicolas Marlet, Wallace Tripp, Claire Wendling, Rik Maki, Ian Gooding, Cynthia Ignacio, just to name a few! And I find other inspiration from going to museums and galleries and even looking at the latest children's books from great storytellers like Dan Santat and Dav Pilkey. Now, going to universities and working with students, I have found inspiration in the young talent coming up in the business.

   I would like to thank my publishers, especially Sean Connelly and Alyss Barraza, my family, my sisters, especially Evaleen for checking all my grammar and spelling, and my friends, for helping me with this book—without your incredible insight and assistance, this book would never have come to be…

   Thank you!

What Is Character Design?

FIGURE 1.1

DOI: 10.1201/9781003599005-1

What Is Character Design?

When we read a book or watch a film or show, we watch characters rise or fall, win or lose, die or kill within the length of that story… we empathize, we identify with the characters as they venture through the story. Characters are who we identify with, who we hate or love.

So when you're looking at great character designs within these projects, what draws you to them? What does it take to make a great character design?

Great character designs are....

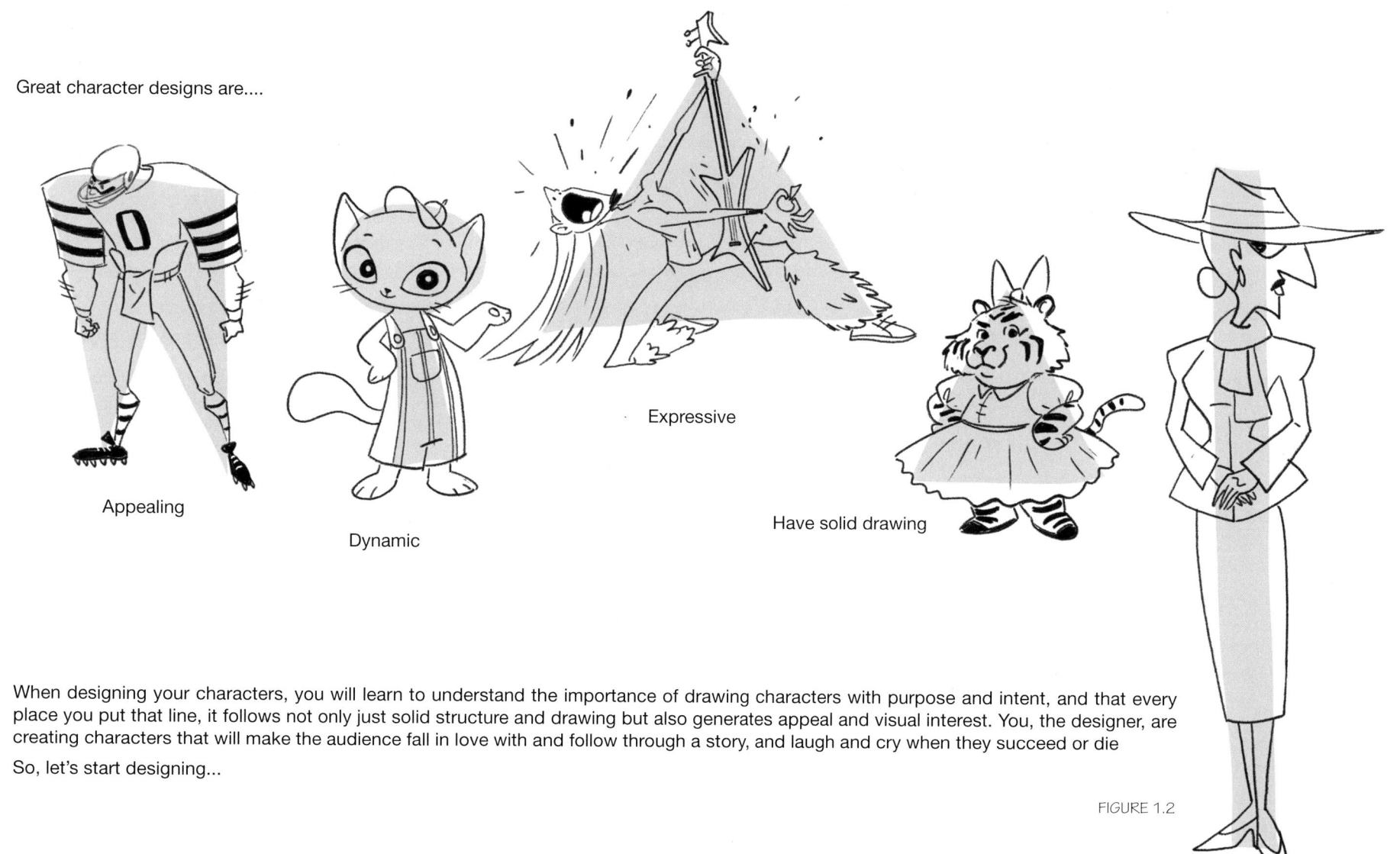

Appealing

Dynamic

Expressive

Have solid drawing

When designing your characters, you will learn to understand the importance of drawing characters with purpose and intent, and that every place you put that line, it follows not only just solid structure and drawing but also generates appeal and visual interest. You, the designer, are creating characters that will make the audience fall in love with and follow through a story, and laugh and cry when they succeed or die

So, let's start designing...

FIGURE 1.2

Drawing with Purpose and Intent

FIGURE 2.1

DOI: 10.1201/9781003599005-2

Drawing with Purpose and Intent

Every line you put down signifies a shape in your character, so it is important to learn to DRAW WITH PURPOSE and INTENT. When you draw the head, for example, be sure to feel the form as you draw…. When you place the details on the head, know exactly where the eyes, the nose, and the mouth are accurately placed on the head. Draw with the knowledge that your character will be that shape and reflect that character's personality, stance, action, etc.

Lines on a character can be subtle so it is important that you understand how these lines work when defining volume, size, shape, etc.

You can start with rough sketches but once you begin tightening down your drawing, you need to know the structure behind the design.

The stages are:

1. Thumbnails, making sure you have good silhouette, shape, and size variation.
2. Rough sketches, tying down the thumbnails into a slightly more clear drawing.
3. Tightening down the sketch … This is where you start to nail down the sketch, where every single line has a purpose to the drawing. You are designing the character overall… as well as designing within that overall design, giving variety and rhythm within those shapes.

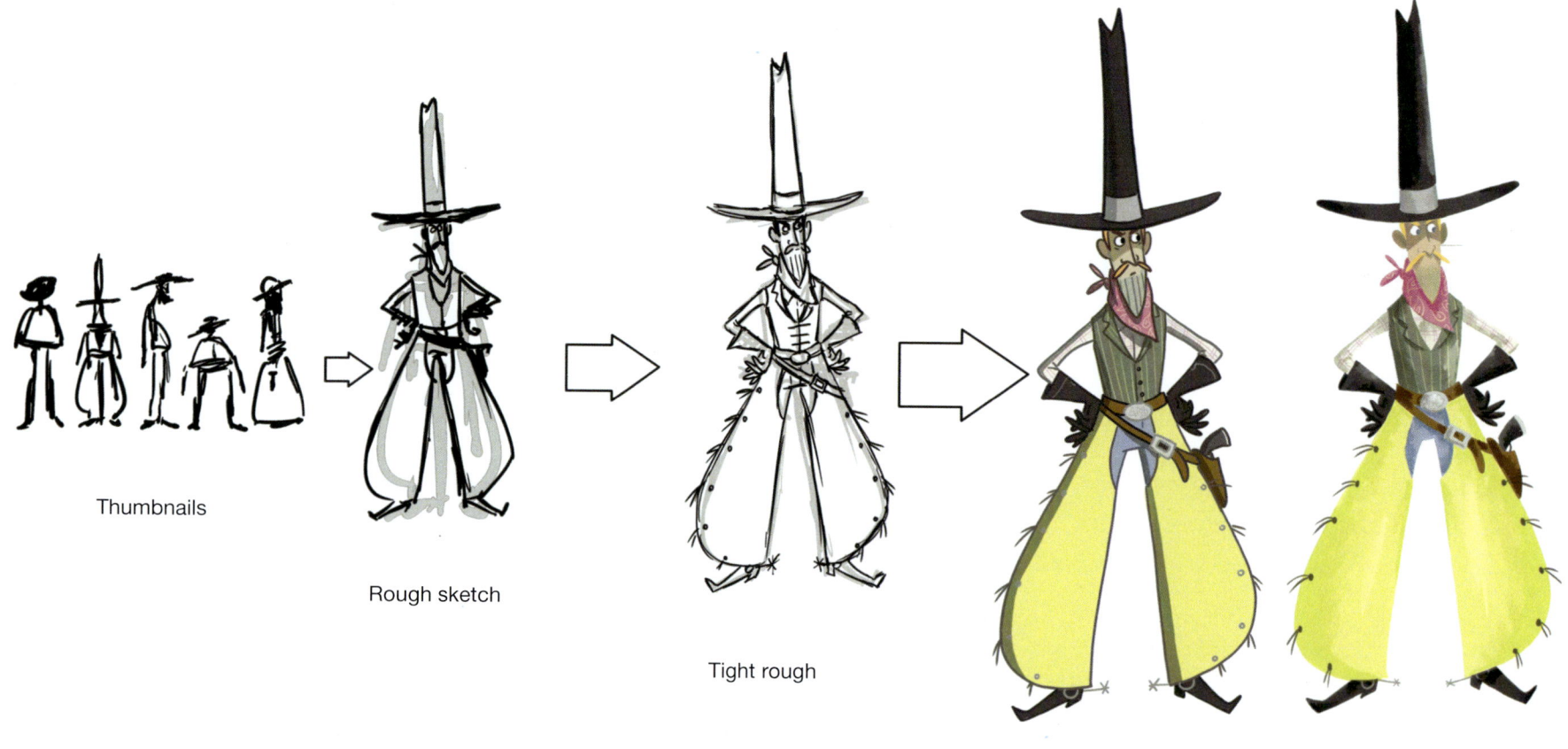

Thumbnails

Rough sketch

Tight rough

Color with clean up line

Color with no line

FIGURE 2.2

Characters and story telling go hand in hand. You, as the character designer, are tasked with designing characters that will move through the story, live, fight, win or lose, survive or die, and all the while, follow the design style and look of the film. Remember that you are working hand in hand with the story... Sometimes, you will find yourself sitting at a large table with story artists, hashing out the characters, figuring out who they are, what makes them tick, what makes them angry, etc. And your character designs will all reflect these personality traits. It will be up to you to draw these characters and ensure that their personalities shine through in your drawings.

Who is your character?

Daring?

Conniving?

FIGURE 2.3

Daydreamy?

Aloof?

Don't make your characters just stand there looking cute and boring – You want to make them breathe, react, fight, laugh, think, etc. All your poses should reflect what these characters think and feel as they travel through the scenes in your story!

How far can you push the designs of your characters and their poses? I find inspiration in other designers and wonderful illustrations. If you can, break limbs, push the limits of gravity and logic to make the greatest design you can draw!

FIGURE 2.4

FIGURE 2.5

Appeal

No matter what character you draw, you need to draw a character that appeals to your audience. The character has to have VISUAL APPEAL, personality, poise… all of which lend itself to appeal to whoever is looking at your story! It is important that you draw the character with a lot of personality, variation of shape and size, show a reflection of proper research and reference… and in the end, just look cool!

Dynamic Drawing: Some Tips!

A basic rule when drawing parts of your character is to never draw shapes that echo the same shapes opposite each other, much like a parenthesis. What you need to do is offset these shapes so those details of your design can look more dynamic.

FIGURE 2.6

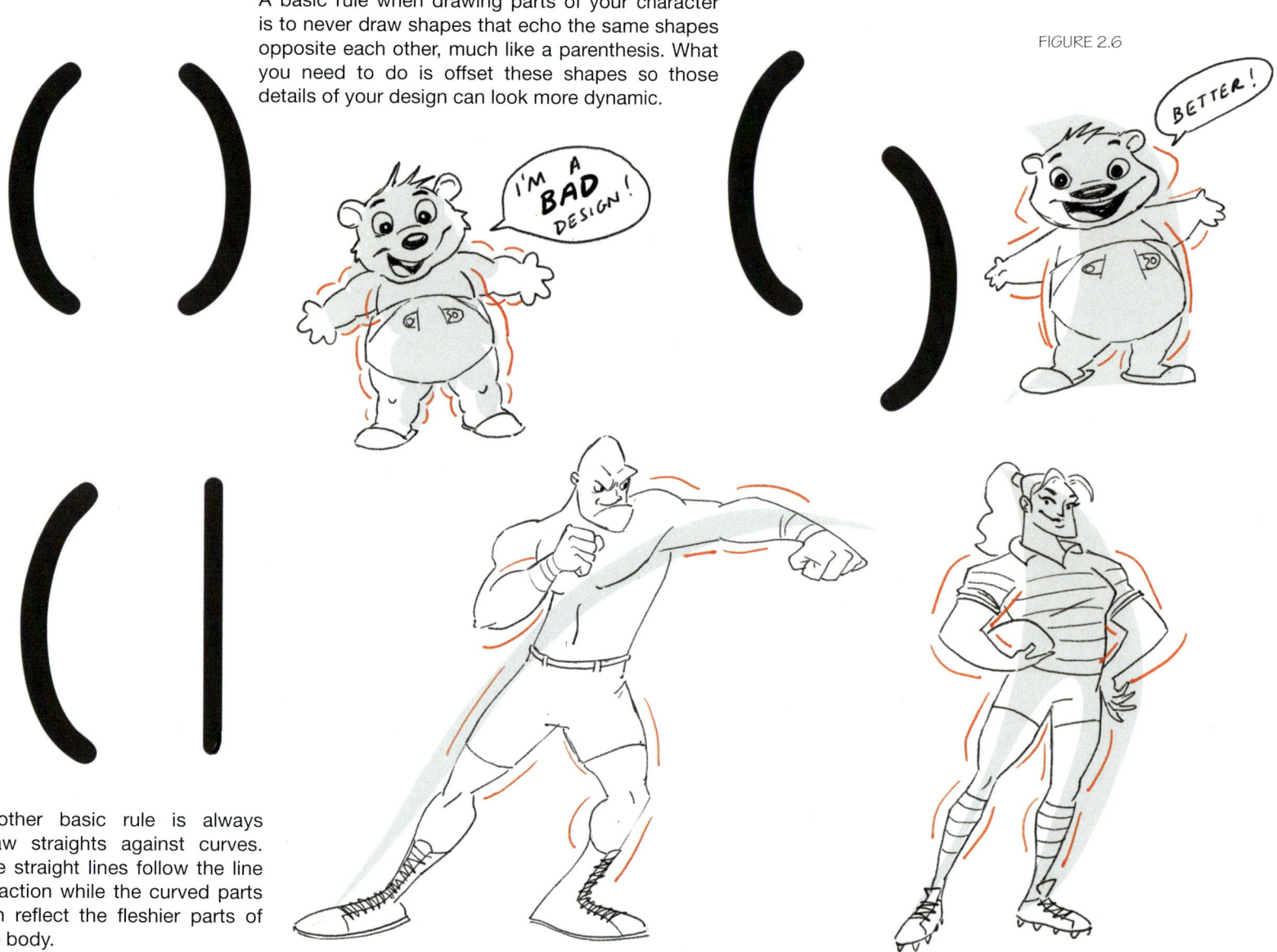

Another basic rule is always draw straights against curves. The straight lines follow the line of action while the curved parts can reflect the fleshier parts of the body.

Solid Drawing

In drawing characters, it is okay to roughly draw your sketches and ideas. But then you must take your designs to the next level, and that involves making sure there is solidity behind your idea. No matter how cartoony or realistic your design is, make sure the shapes are solid, connect accurately together, and are drawn in perspective accurately, or else your design will fall apart.

So… know your shapes, understand the plane changes in your shapes, and be confident in their connectivity to each other to ensure the solidity of your drawing!

FIGURE 2.7

Expressive Characters

Character design isn't just about designing a character that's cool. It's about working with your story crew, your director, and other designers. It's about designing WHO your characters are, WHY your characters act the way they do, and WHAT motivates your characters to act the way they do. The goal is to bring the character to life and, make them breathe on a 2D or 3D surface. In the visual development process, you could be spending a long time with a variety of characters, working with an ever-changing story; it is your job to discover a unique character that the audience will relate to and fall in love with on screen. Your character can be subtle or broad in their emotions but above all, their expressions must be CLEAR. Keep in mind that your audience will look at your drawing and get a sense of who that character is within a split second! So it is up to you to draw that expression clearly and expressively.

So, let's begin the process of designing characters…

FIGURE 2.8

Thumbnails

FIGURE 3.1

DOI: 10.1201/9781003599005-3

Thumbnails

FIGURE 3.2

What is a thumbnail? It's a rough sketch about the size of your thumb! When you're conceptualizing your characters, you should figure out what these characters are shaped like, in the broadest of terms, and how they fit in comparison to each other. You should have some idea of what form your character is, and from there, you can pull and push your shapes. For example, our character, Mary, is a human, so we shall start with the humanoid form and then we will push and pull our shapes. Be sure to think when you are doing your thumbnails, think SHAPE, SILHOUETTE, SIZE.

Use a nice THICK pen! Be doing so, you AVOID getting into details that you don't need to deal with at this very early stage of development.

My concept: An Idea I springboarded from "Mary Had a Little Lamb."

Mary (humanoid)

As I am doodling/ scribbling, I am thinking about WHO this Mary is, what SHAPE she is, WHERE she lives, WHAT TIME PERIOD she lives in, and what's going on during that place and time. Even if the time and place are fantasy, you can still come up with ideas that are based on real-life events, past and present.

The development process of building characters is fluid and can change at any time, when you continue your research.

One of Mary's Pals – a male humanoid

The Lamb

SCRIBBLE!

DOODLING IS YOUR
BEST FRIEND!

FIGURE 3.3

I DON'T KNOW!

The thumbnail phase of visual development is truly the "I don't know" phase, because you really don't know what you're going to find in your thumbnails! It is important to stay loose and keep an open mind. Embrace the unknown when you doodle and scribble. You will find new shapes that you've never drawn before and come up with more interesting designs in the process.

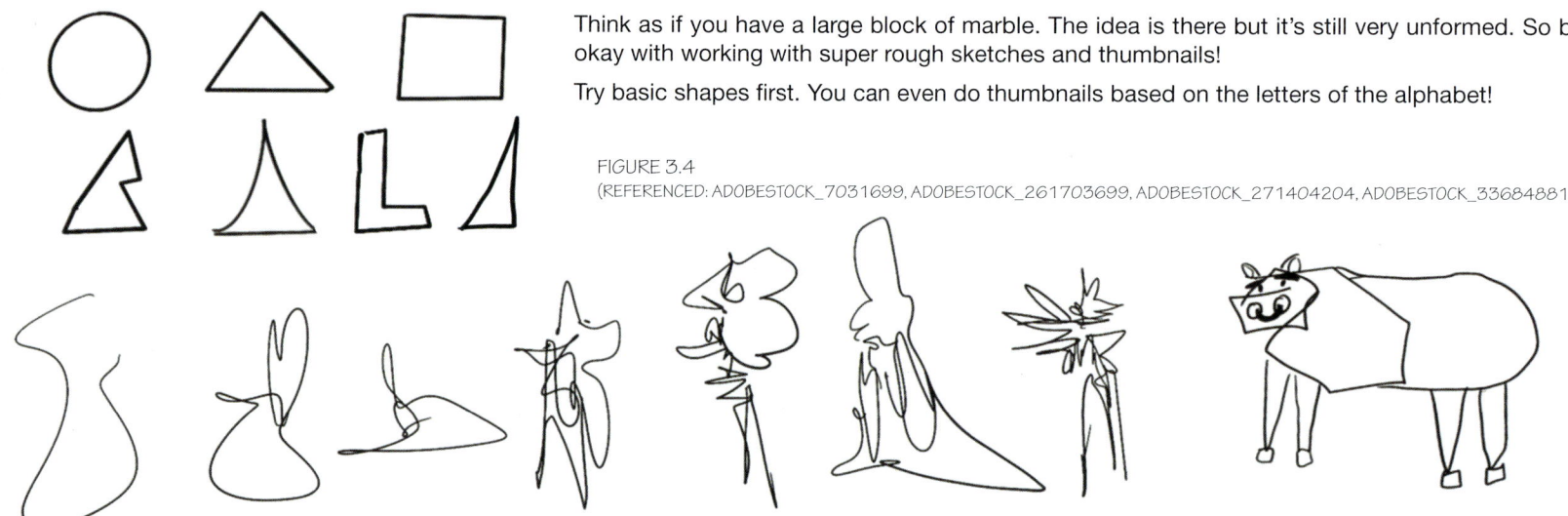

Think as if you have a large block of marble. The idea is there but it's still very unformed. So be okay with working with super rough sketches and thumbnails!

Try basic shapes first. You can even do thumbnails based on the letters of the alphabet!

FIGURE 3.4
(REFERENCED: ADOBESTOCK_7031699, ADOBESTOCK_261703699, ADOBESTOCK_271404204, ADOBESTOCK_336848818)

You can find shapes in nature as well… Interesting shapes can help push designs to the limit!

OR… try doing blobs…

See what shapes you can discover! The point of doing this, is to get out of your comfort zone, push shapes and silhouette. You will find that doing thumbnails first will improve your designing exponentially.

Sometimes you can work on thumbnails, and work with values and variations on shapes that way.

Some more ideas for Mary…

Some more ideas for Mary's pal…

Some more ideas for the bad guy…

FIGURE 3.5

Now that you've done your thumbnails, take one from each group of characters and put them all together in a lineup. Size them up or down so you can get a nice size variation of them. They should be hopefully distinctive enough in their rough overall shapes.

FIGURE 3.6

Here are my thumbnails…

You don't have to stick to these thumbnails too tightly… there may be an aspect of your other thumbnails you like! Always keep that open mind… You're still in development. Your characters will evolve...

Once you blow up your thumbnails, you can start doing tight roughs, going over your designs roughly and loosely. You don't have to be married to your thumbnails. This is truly an early stage of your development of characters. Stay loose, stay open to any other ideas you discover!

As you begin fleshing out these characters, be sure to add some EXPRESSION, APPEAL, DYNAMISM, and STRUCTURE to your drawings!

FIGURE 3.7

These are some more thumbnails I've worked through, after looking at fashion magazines and other sources of inspiration. Looking at visual references helps inspire different shapes and size variations in your thumbnail doodles!

From this stage of doodling and scribbling, start carving out and sketching rough ideas for your designs. Stay broad and rough… Working out the design within the design, i.e., details in the clothing or the face, etc., will come at the next stages.

FIGURE 3.8

We will begin fleshing out our characters… Here are some basic drawing tips to drawing your characters… Keep it rough! You really don't want to set things in stone just yet – You're still very early in the development stage of your characters and are getting to know your characters.

Stances

Do yourself a favor and DON'T stand your character like a robot! I see this pose a lot:

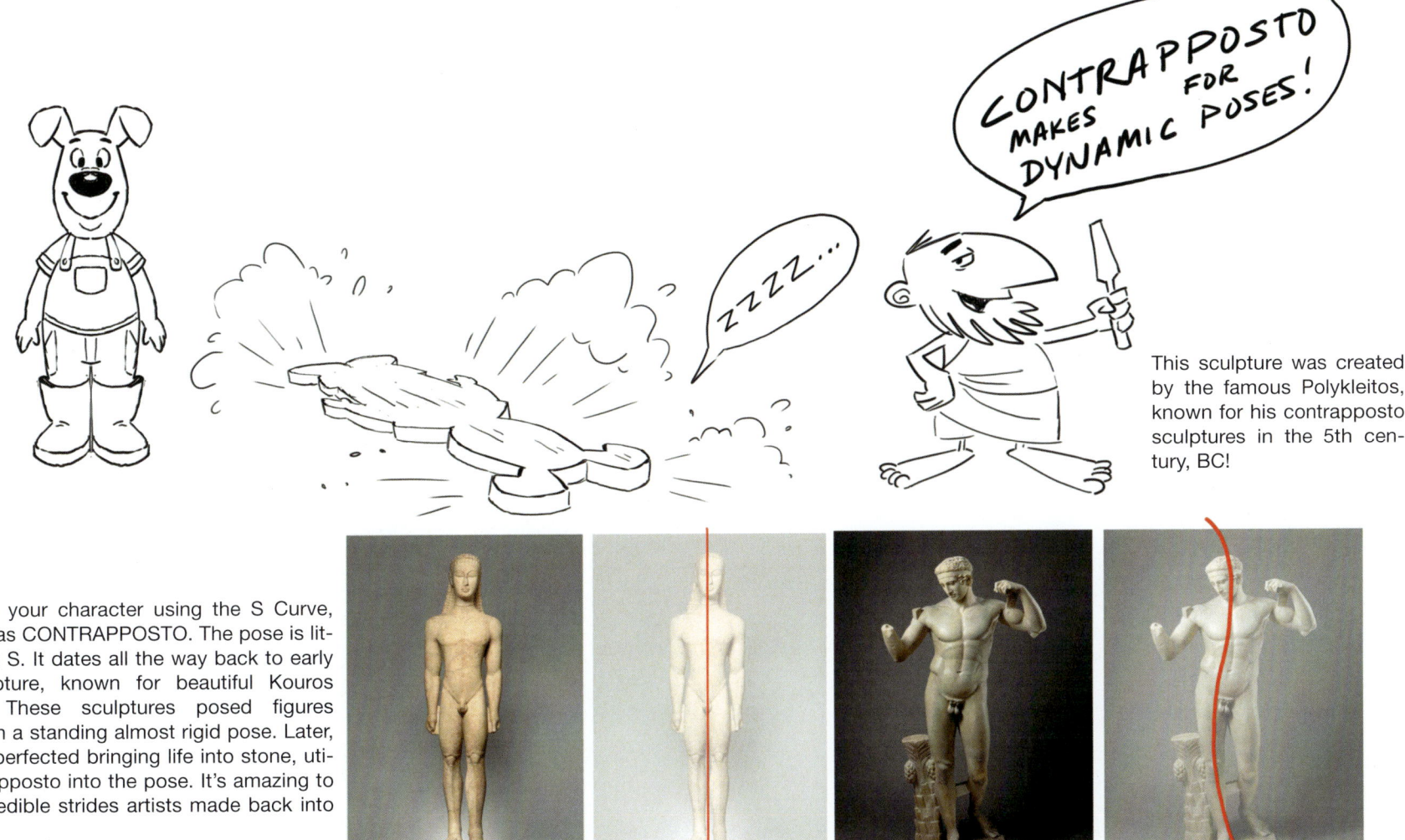

This sculpture was created by the famous Polykleitos, known for his contrapposto sculptures in the 5th century, BC!

Bring life to your character using the S Curve, also known as CONTRAPPOSTO. The pose is literally like an S. It dates all the way back to early Greek sculpture, known for beautiful Kouros sculptures. These sculptures posed figures straight up in a standing almost rigid pose. Later, the Greeks perfected bringing life into stone, utilizing contrapposto into the pose. It's amazing to see the incredible strides artists made back into those days!

FIGURE 3.9
(REFERENCED: METMUSEUM.ORG/ART/COLLECTION/SEARCH/251838; METMUSEUM.ORG/ART/COLLECTION/SEARCH/263370)

Anatomy and the Importance of Figure Drawing in Character Design

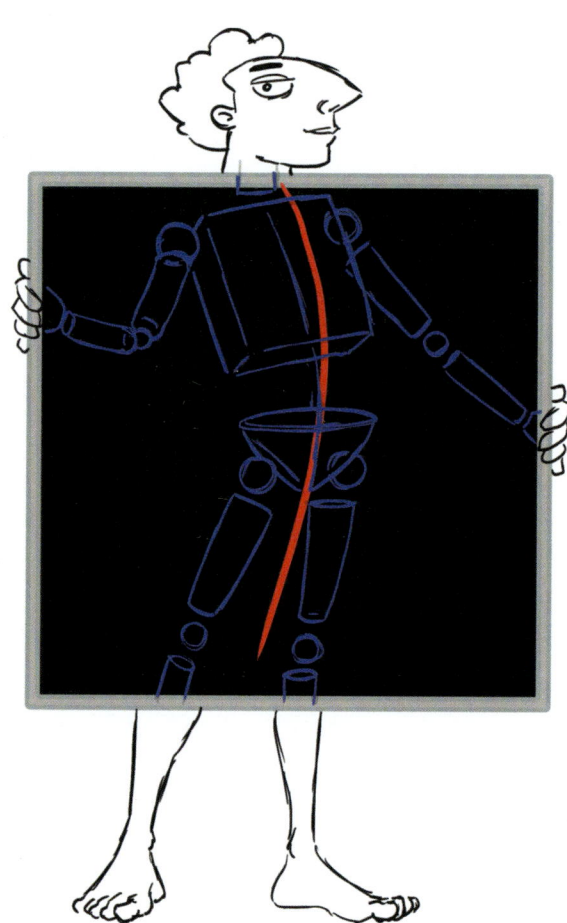

4

FIGURE 4.1

DOI: 10.1201/9781003599005-4

Anatomy and the Importance of Figure Drawing in Character Design

Figure Drawing and how it relates to Character Design

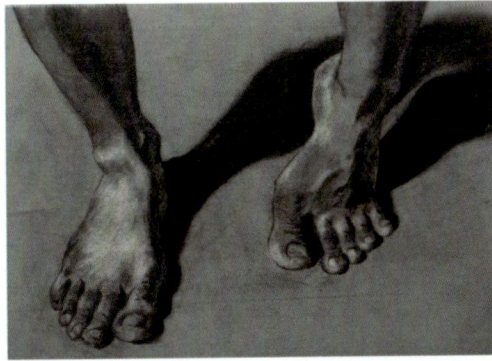

FIGURE 4.2
(REFERENCED: WWW.METMUSEUM.ORG/ART/COLLECTION/
SEARCH/338049, WWW.METMUSEUM.ORG/ART/
COLLECTION/SEARCH/459459)

It is so important to take figure drawing classes! Why? It will help to know how limbs connect, how the nose fits on the face, etc. It will show how musculature can inform your character design. It will show how to draw drapery and how to draw clothing on figures.

I was taught to FEEL THE FORM as I did my figure drawing, and I absolutely feel that is true! As you draw your character designs, you can also feel the form, feel the flow of your designs, and make some truly dynamic and appealing characters.

If you do figure drawing, you get a feel for the forms of the figure, such as how limbs and clothes wrap around the figure, From there, you can caricature and still capture the essence and feel of your reference.

FIGURE 4.3

Caricaturing can be difficult! Here's an approach…

The Alphabet Method

Using the shapes of the letters of the alphabet, you can derive interesting shapes to create unique looks and designs.

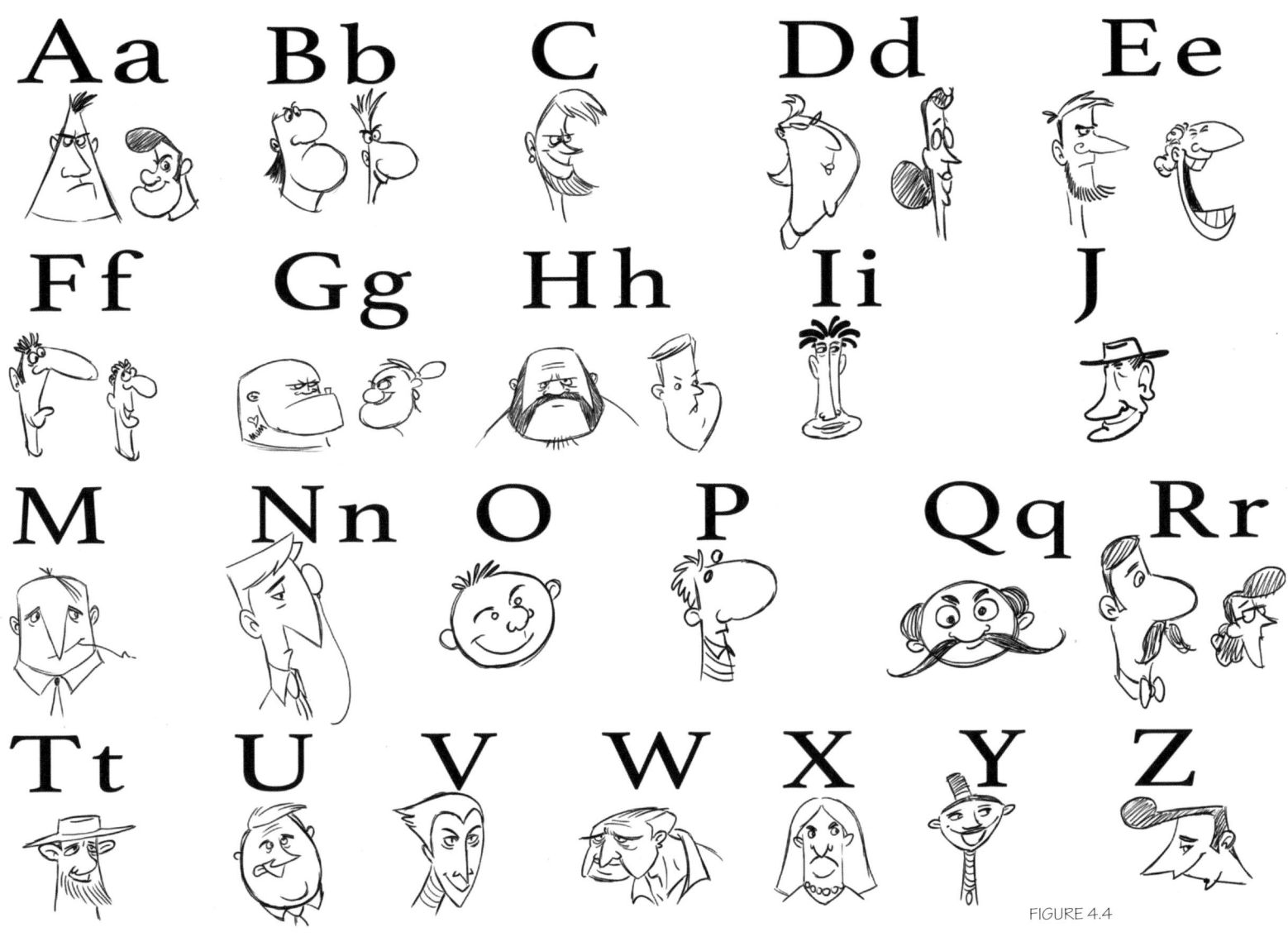

FIGURE 4.4

Eyes, Nose, Lips

Lots of folks have a tough time drawing facial details, such as the eyes, nose, and lips. It's difficult to figure out the structure of these parts, so I'm going to tackle some of these details here.

The eyeballs are literally just that... a ball! That ball sits inside two soft lids that WRAP around this ball, from the top and bottom of that ball when it opens and closes.

Now you can draw eyes in pretty much any roundish type of shape, but just know, it still wraps around a ROUNDISH shape that is the eyeball.

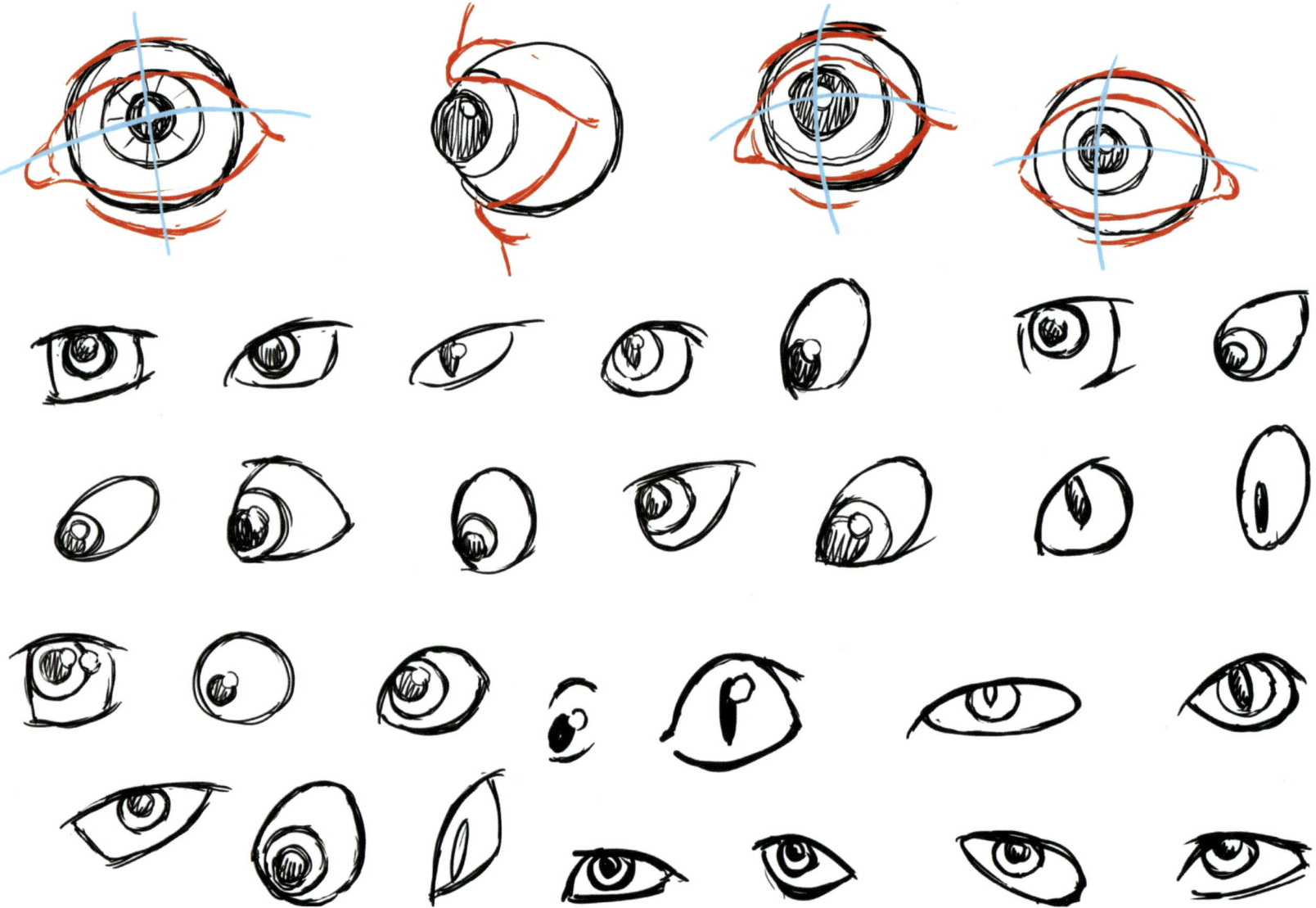

FIGURE 4.5

The Mask

Let's look at the MASK. Every face has a "mask" surrounding the eyes, the eyebrows, and the bags under the eyes.

Think of it like it's a superhero mask. Every time your character looks in a direction, those eyebrows squash and stretch and help with the facial expressions of your character.

FIGURE 4.6

The Nose

This nose is like a triangular wedge with two half globes on each side (the nostrils). The nose in animation can come in different shapes and sizes. And there are shortcuts to drawing the nose. You just have to understand the shape from different viewpoints, and then you'll be good to go!

Now be sure to place the nose right in between the mask area and keep it centered!

What about the animal muzzle? The rule still applies...

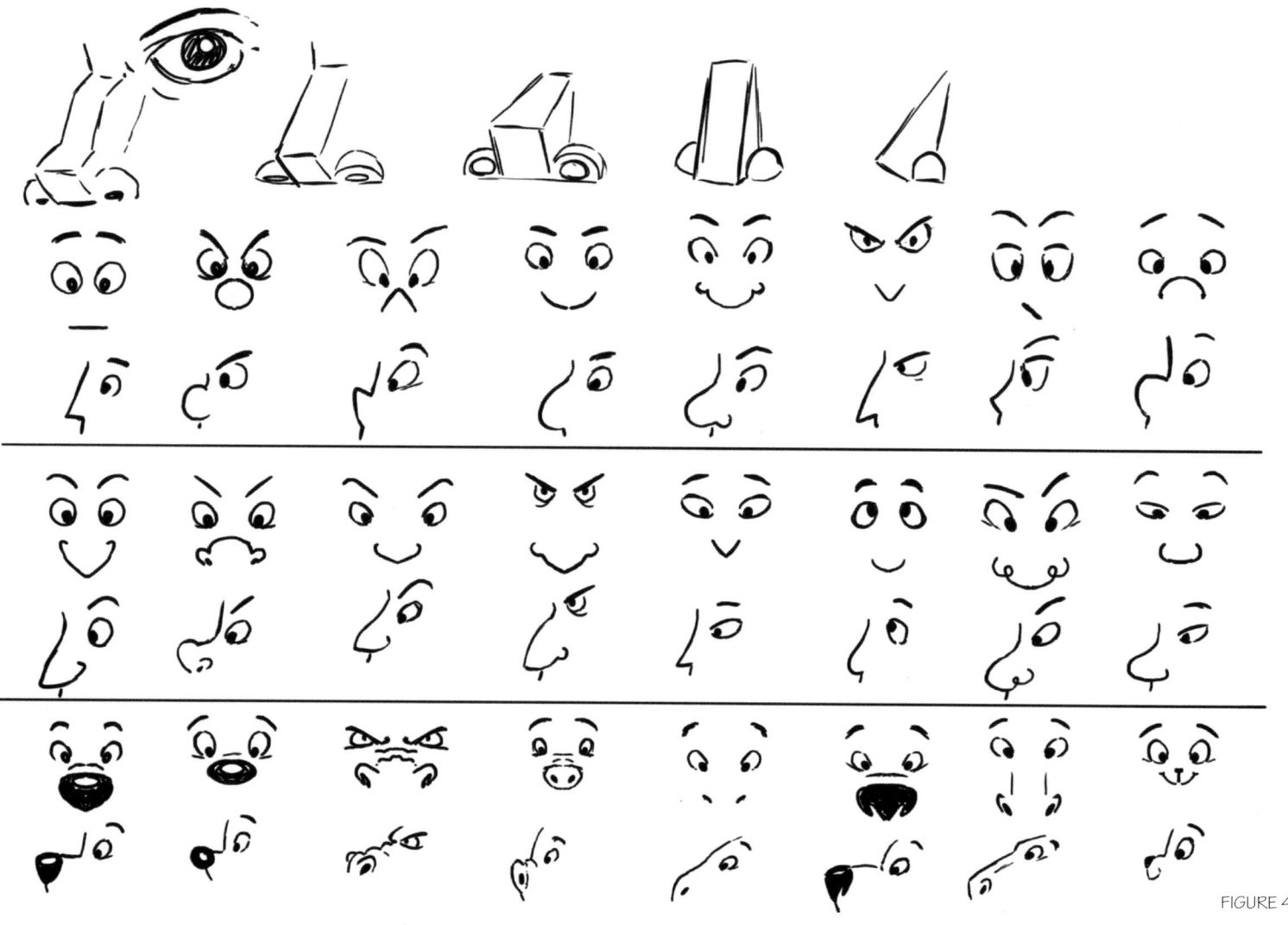

FIGURE 4.7

The Lips

The lips, like the eyes and nose are symmetrical! The lips can have multiple shapes so go nuts! When you turn it, the shape is the same, just cut it in half! If you add facial hair, it is also symmetrical on the face! Remember, we are an amalgam of two cells put together... so everything on the human is the same on one side as on the other.

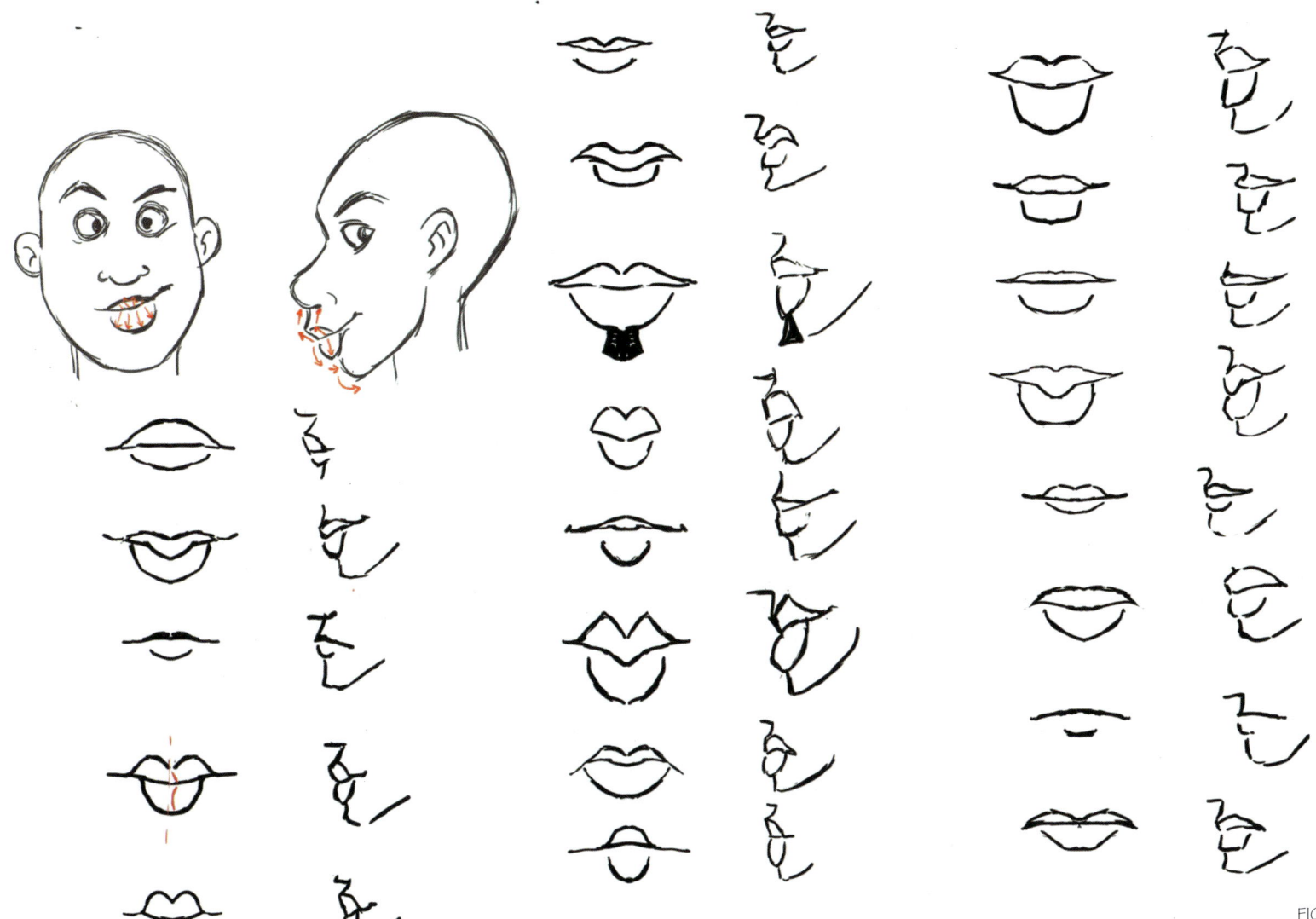

FIGURE 4.8

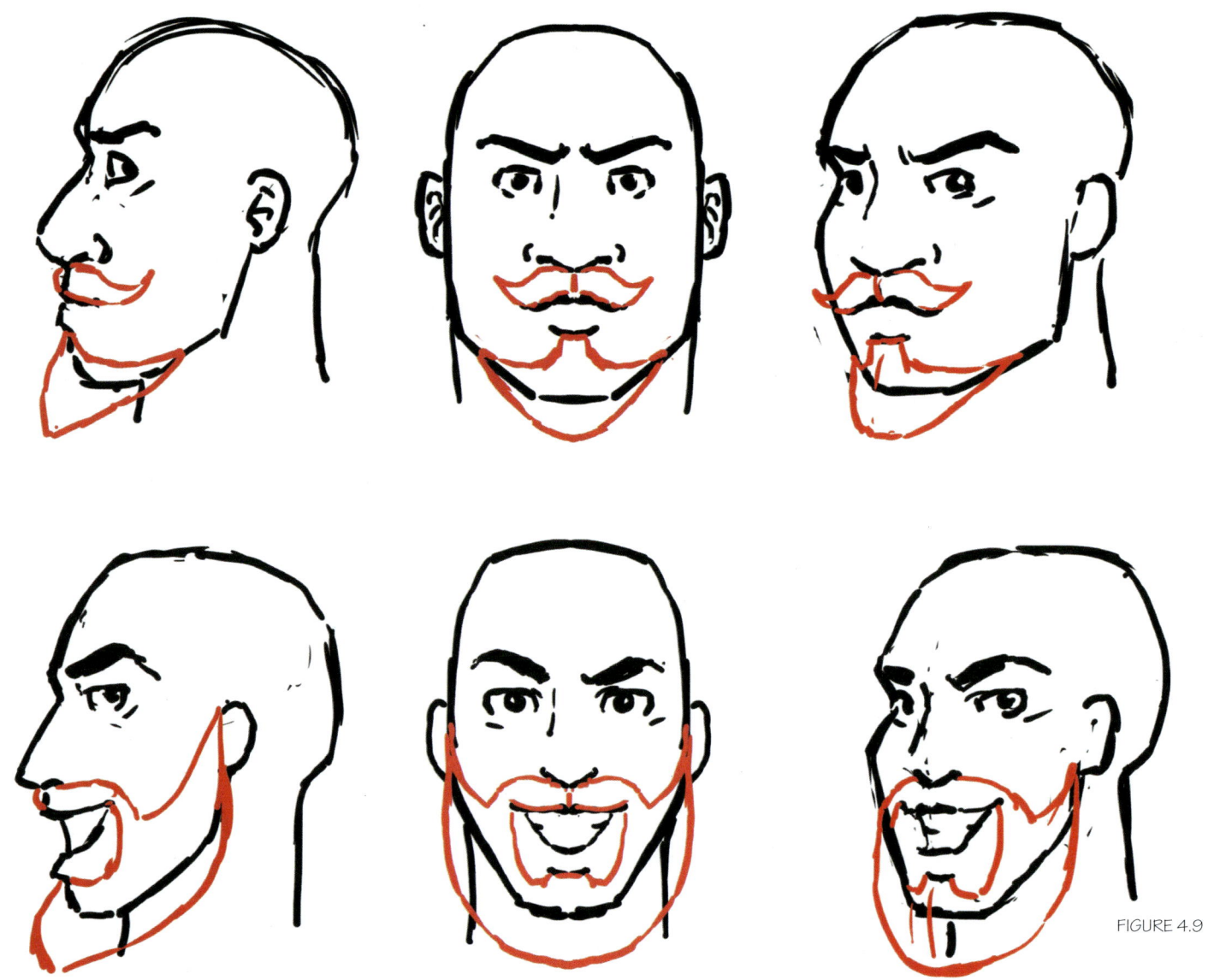

FIGURE 4.9

Facial hair is one of those things that wrap around the muzzle symmetrically. Remember, it is a shape, and it can be as fun and whimsical and as creative as you like! Facial hair, like head hair, is an expression of who that character is.

Facial hair grows from the ears, runs down the jawline and above and around the mouth. Everyone has a different pattern of growth along the muzzle, which can dictate your design. Remember also that facial hair has volume, so be sure to design that volume on the muzzle accordingly.

It may be a good idea to draw the face naked first and then add the facial hair along the muzzle.

FIGURE 4.10

Let's Look at the Face!

If you put a human skull on any design, you can caricature ANY part of the human face! The challenge is to balance it all together to make a face that is visually interesting and unique. Look at your reference, see what the most unique aspect of their face and caricature is, but also balance it with another part of the face being smaller or larger...

So – is the nose big? Balance it with small eyes, perhaps... Or, are the lips large? Balance it with a thin nose or small eyes... If everything on your face is big, you run the risk of making the face look odd.

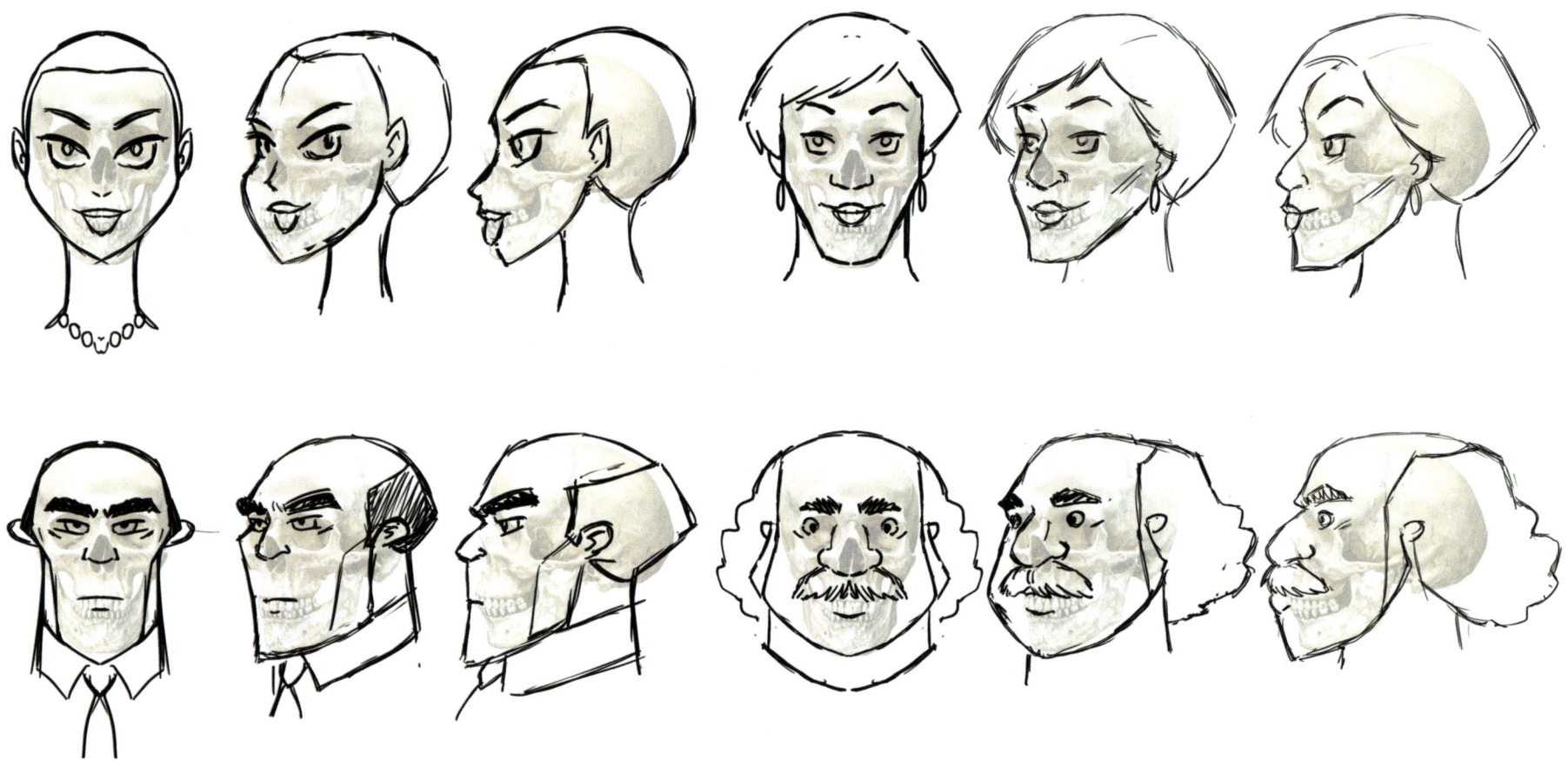

FIGURE 4.11
(REFERENCED: ADOBESTOCK_86706454, ADOBESTOCK_87893193, ADOBESTOCK_89126666)

Hair is just a shape! When you turn the head of a character, you can fudge certain perspectives as long as it looks appealing and follows the original shape.

FIGURE 4.12

Hats

Be sure to follow visual references when you're drawing hats! They, like everything else in design, can be crazy but they still follow a basic shape, so no matter how tall your hat is, or how wide the brim, understand the perspective of where it sits on the head and how it looks when you turn that character.

For example, baseball hats can look odd when drawn at a straightforward angle.

When drawing hats, be sure to draw through your shapes!

This shape for a cowboy hat is a cheat so you can cheat the shape of this hat and still turn it!

FIGURE 4.13

Hands

Hands are a big part of design! Hands allow for acting and expression in your character, so it is imperative that you know how to draw hands effectively. As always, it's great to look at the figure drawing books from Andrew Loomis and Bridgman for reference... and then simplify them to the design style of your choice for your characters.

Think of the fingers on the hand as 5 little tube like characters bunched together! They all move independently and in different directions.

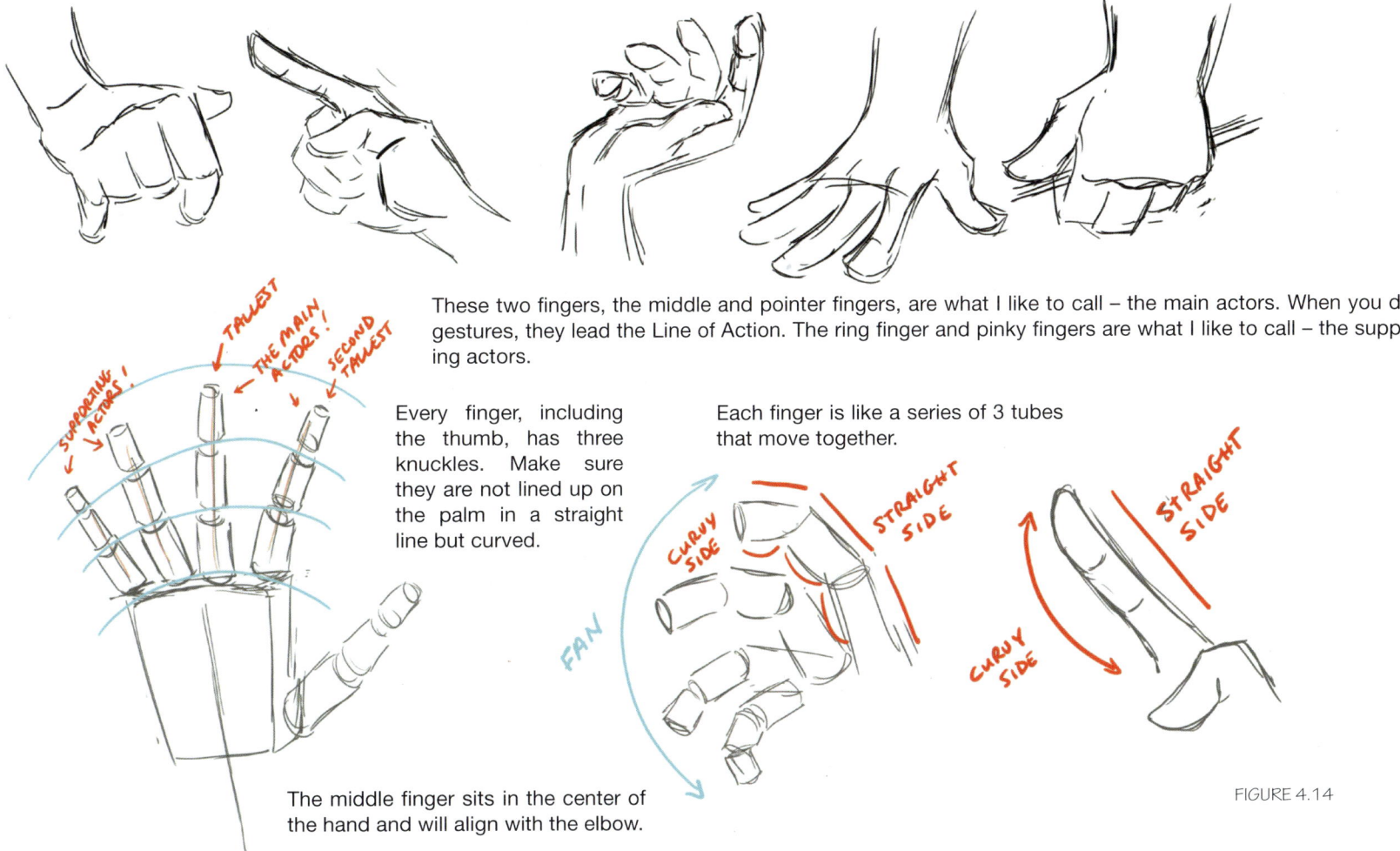

These two fingers, the middle and pointer fingers, are what I like to call – the main actors. When you draw gestures, they lead the Line of Action. The ring finger and pinky fingers are what I like to call – the supporting actors.

Every finger, including the thumb, has three knuckles. Make sure they are not lined up on the palm in a straight line but curved.

Each finger is like a series of 3 tubes that move together.

The middle finger sits in the center of the hand and will align with the elbow.

FIGURE 4.14

Straights vs. Curves

The back side of each finger is straight, and the inside fleshy part of each finger is curved. So, always draw straights vs. curves when drawing fingers.

Hand Turnarounds

It is imperative to learn to turn hands in a full turnaround. A good start is to draw a mitten first, draw the center line through the mitten to find the middle finger. I like to draw the middle and the largest finger first, then pointer fingers, then draw the supporting actors – the ring finger, the third largest, and the pinky and smallest finger last.

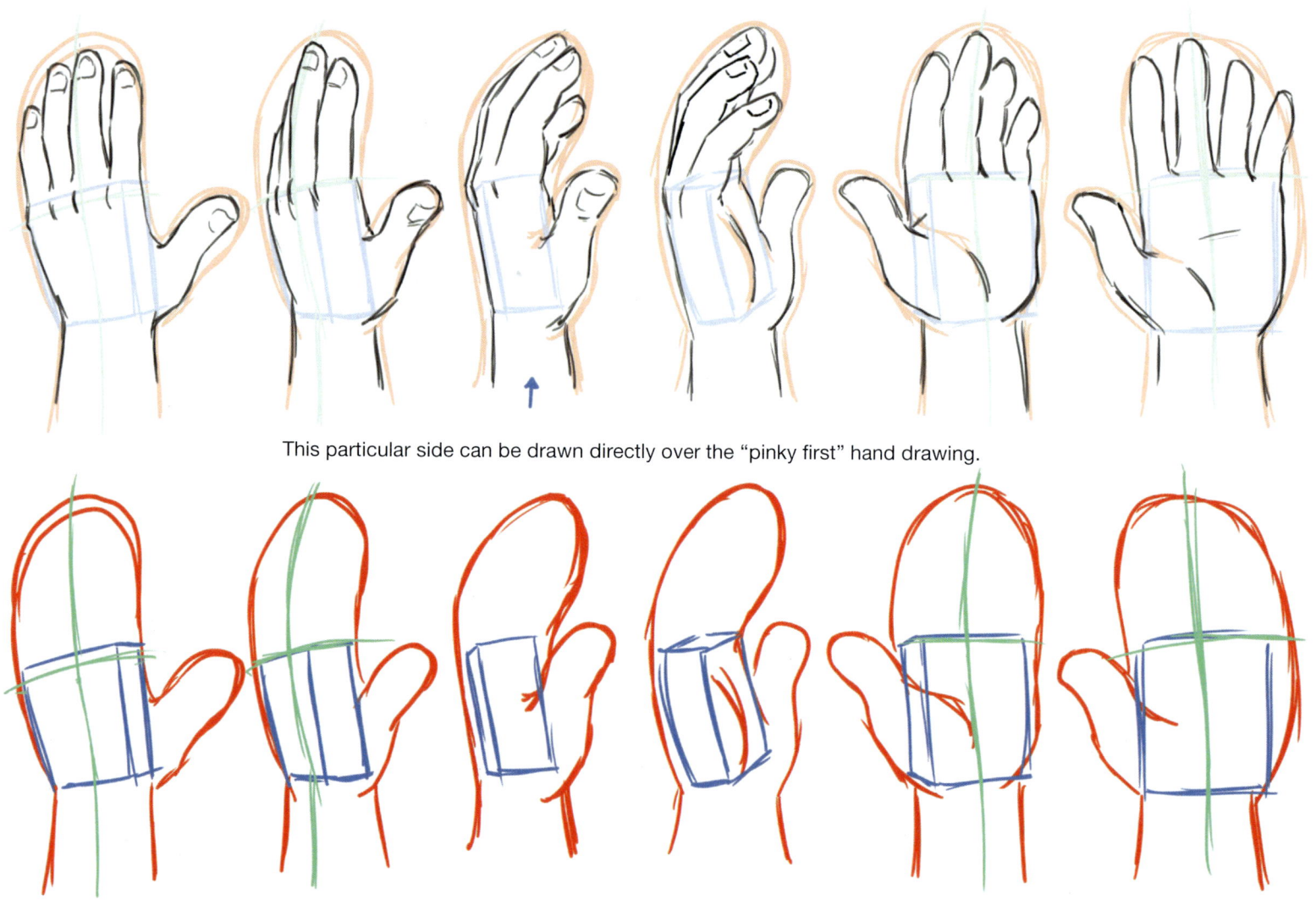

This particular side can be drawn directly over the "pinky first" hand drawing.

FIGURE 4.15

Knowing how to turn hands is critical and useful in doing the full-body turnarounds.

FIGURE 4.16

Draw Space - Draw your ideas and sketches here!

The Mitten Approach

The middle finger and knuckle are the tallest and thickest of the four long fingers.

Split the hand in half. That is where your middle finger sits in the mitten.

The fingers and the knuckle area are curved, not straight! Draw the mitten and fit all those fingers in there, as if wearing the mitten.

The knuckles are a tad lower than the thumb.

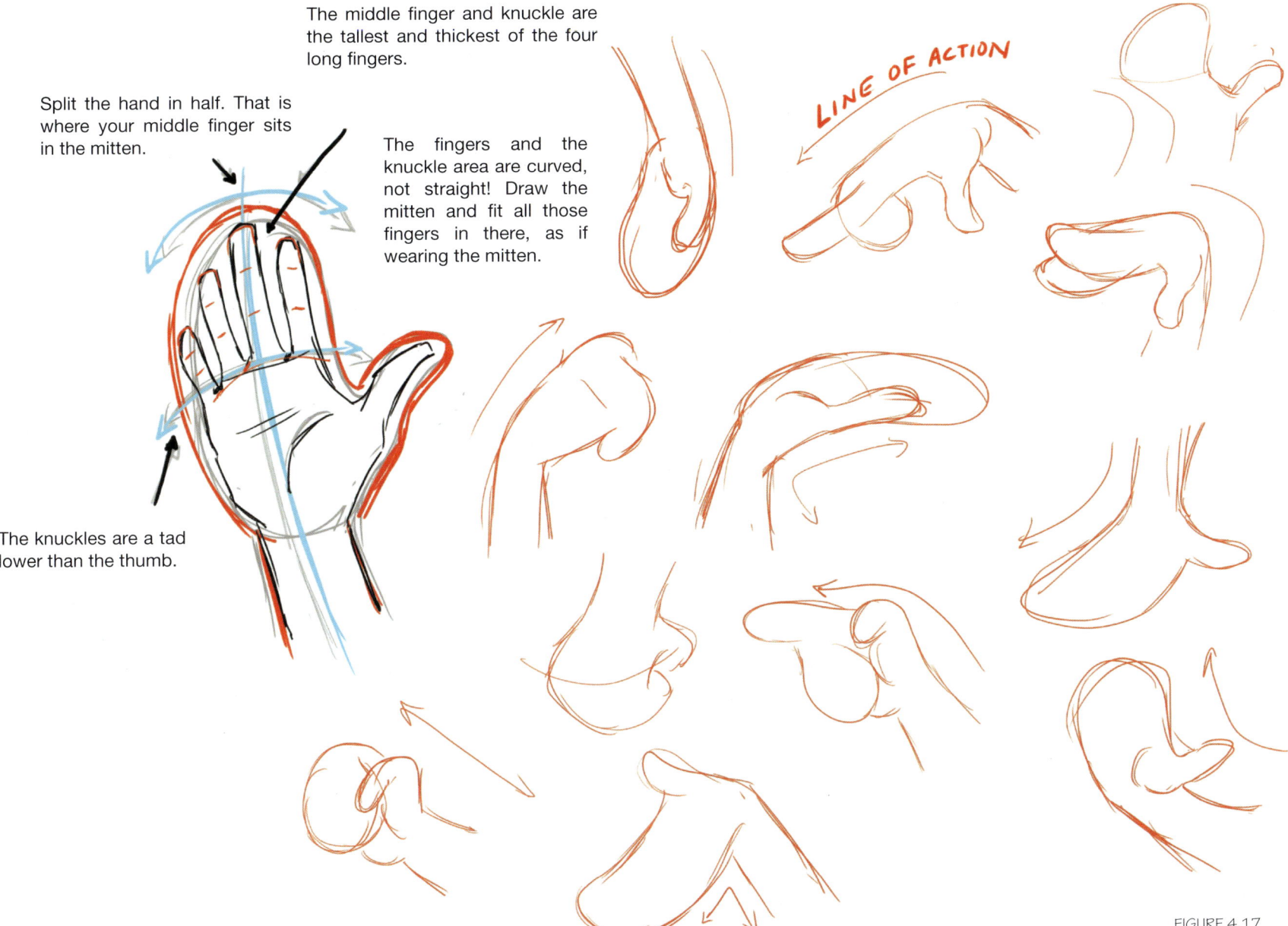

LINE OF ACTION

FIGURE 4.17

Try it! Use the Mitten Approach to draw some hands...

The Mitten Approach

A semi-realistic approach of drawing hands

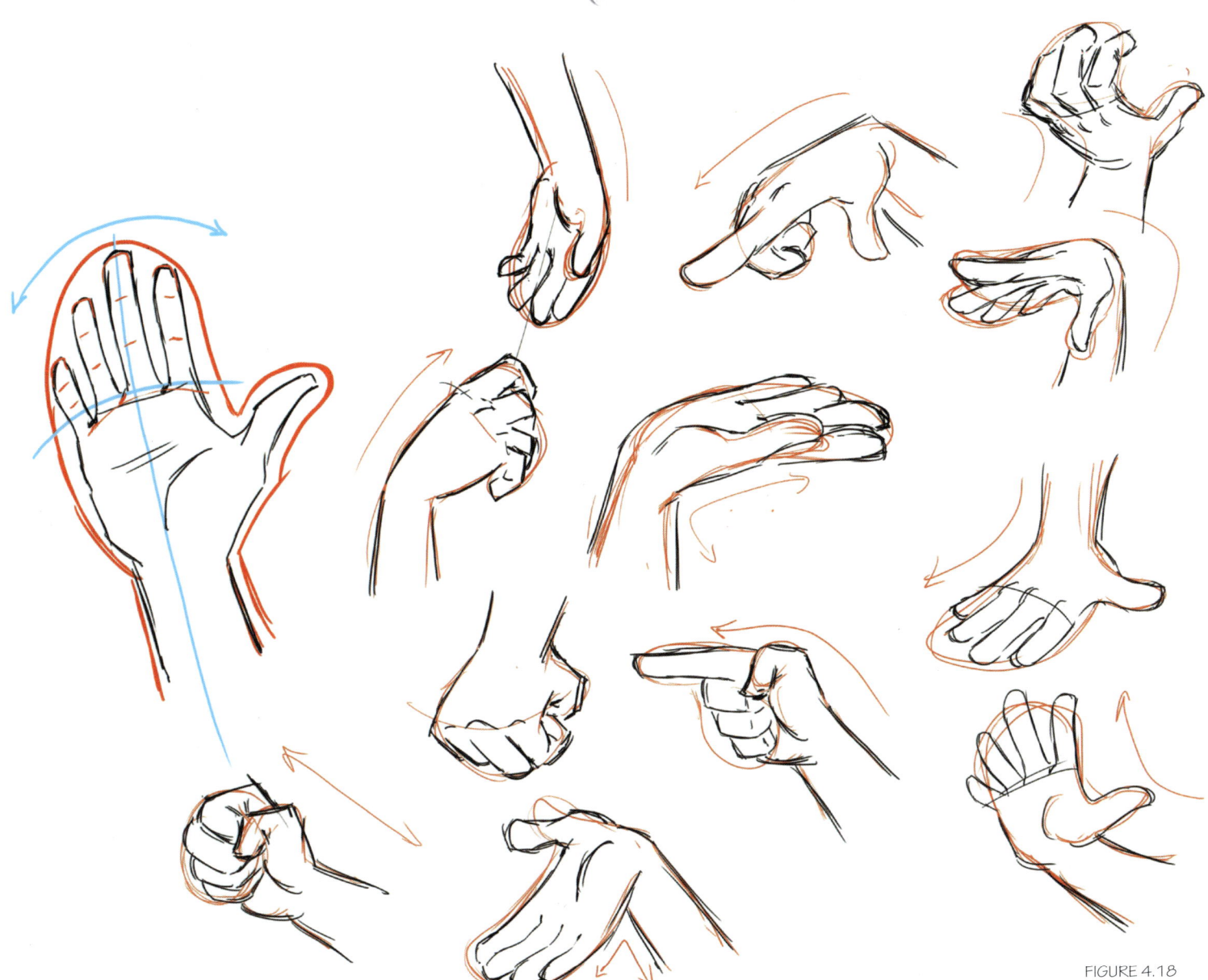

FIGURE 4.18

Now use the Mitten Approach to draw some cartoony hands

You can even use the mitten approach on cartoony hands too…

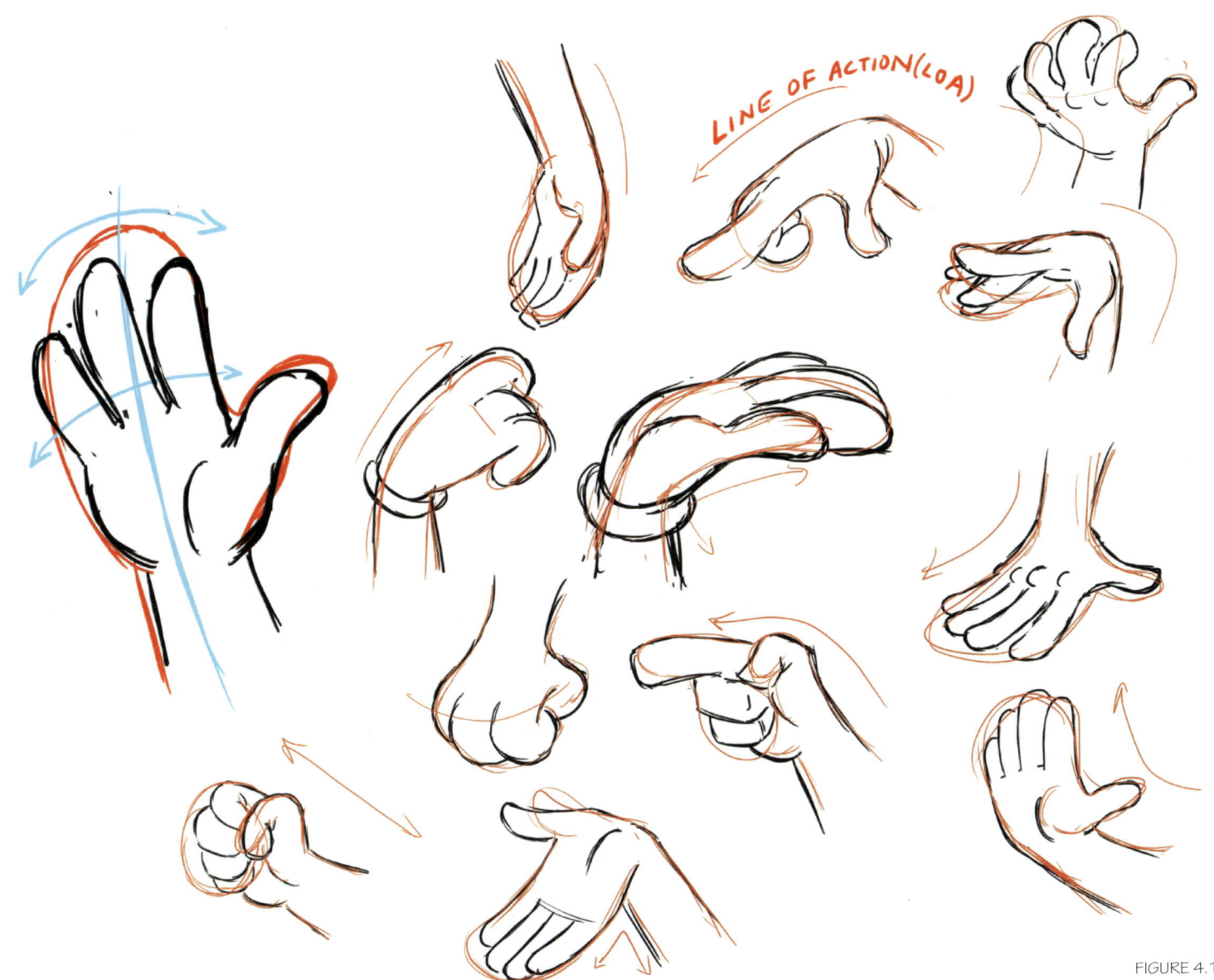

LINE OF ACTION (LOA)

FIGURE 4.19

Use the Stick Finger Approach to draw realistic looking hands.

The Stick Finger Approach

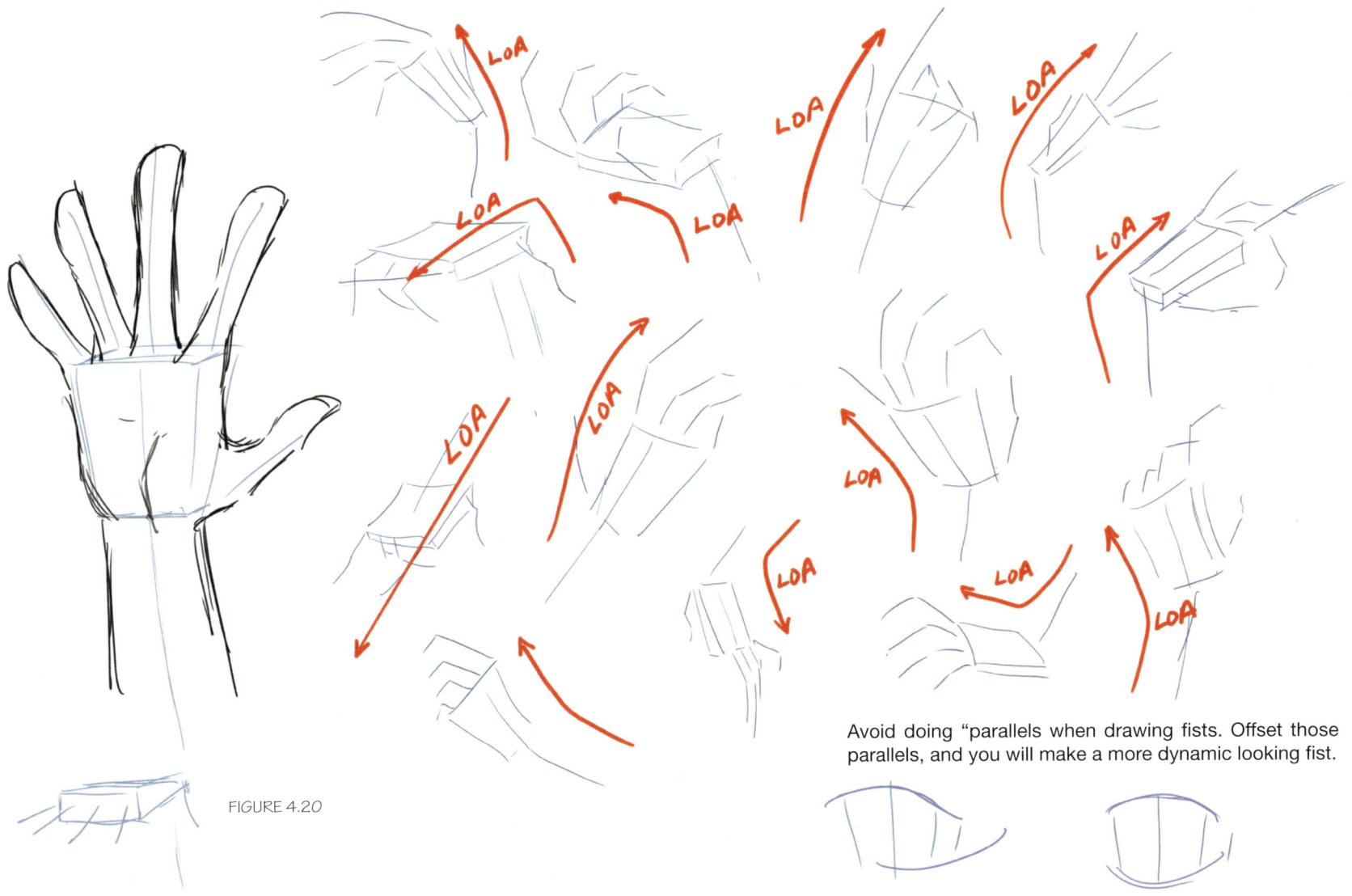

FIGURE 4.20

Avoid doing "parallels when drawing fists. Offset those parallels, and you will make a more dynamic looking fist.

I also use a stick figure method, especially with more difficult poses. I draw the finger gestures as sticks, all sitting on a narrow box. From there, I know where to draw my tubes and fingers!

Use the Stick Finger Approach to draw some realistic looking hands.

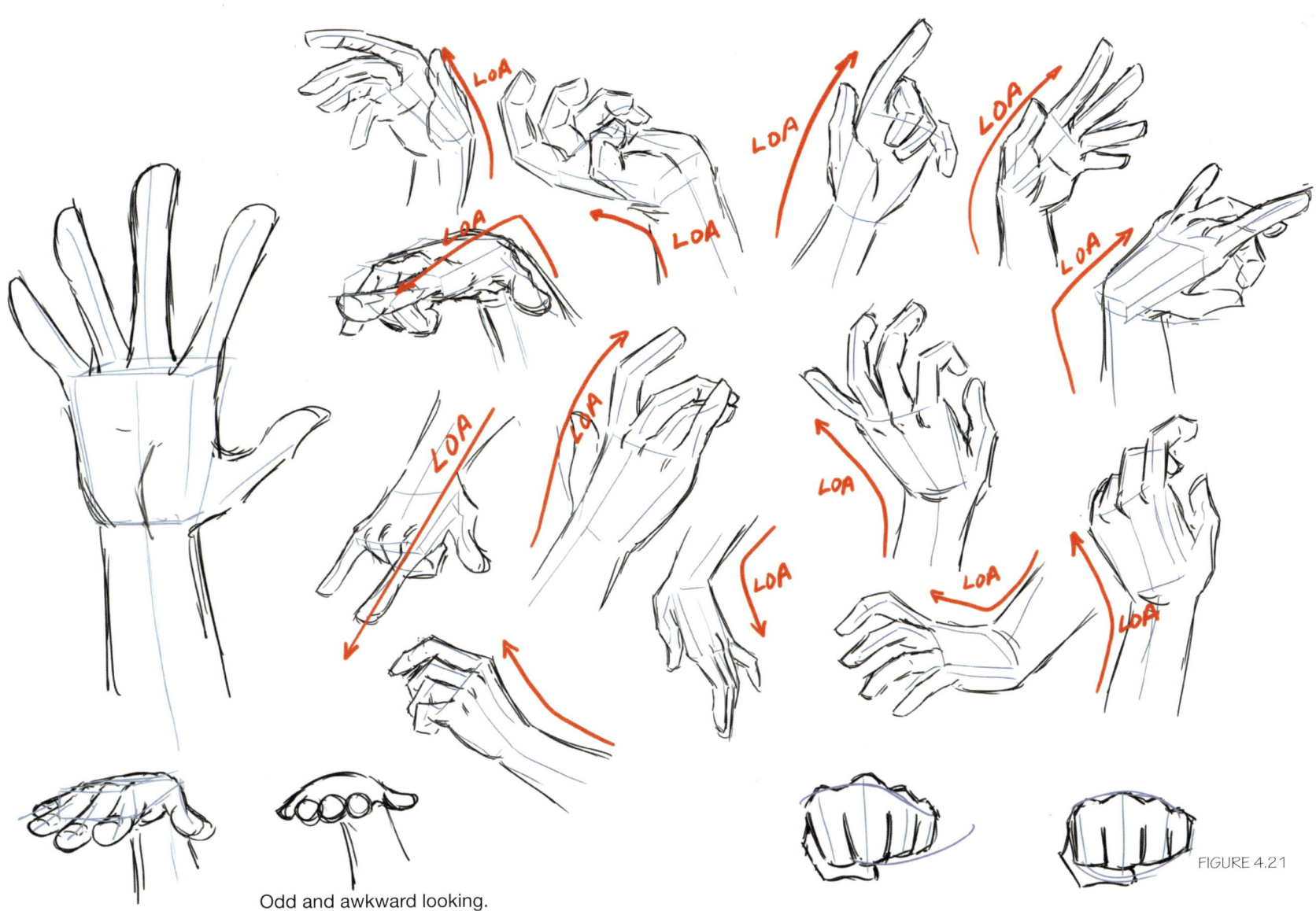

Odd and awkward looking.

FIGURE 4.21

I usually don't put fingers pointing directly to the camera, as it looks odd. In photographs, one can look at this photo and see that this pose works well, but that is because there are millions of colors one sees in a photo. In a drawing, one has limited numbers of colors and it will look odd and awkward looking. It is best to move fingers off to one side or another

Use the Stick Finger Approach to draw some realistic-looking hands…

You can also use the stick figure approach on doing cartoony hands as well.

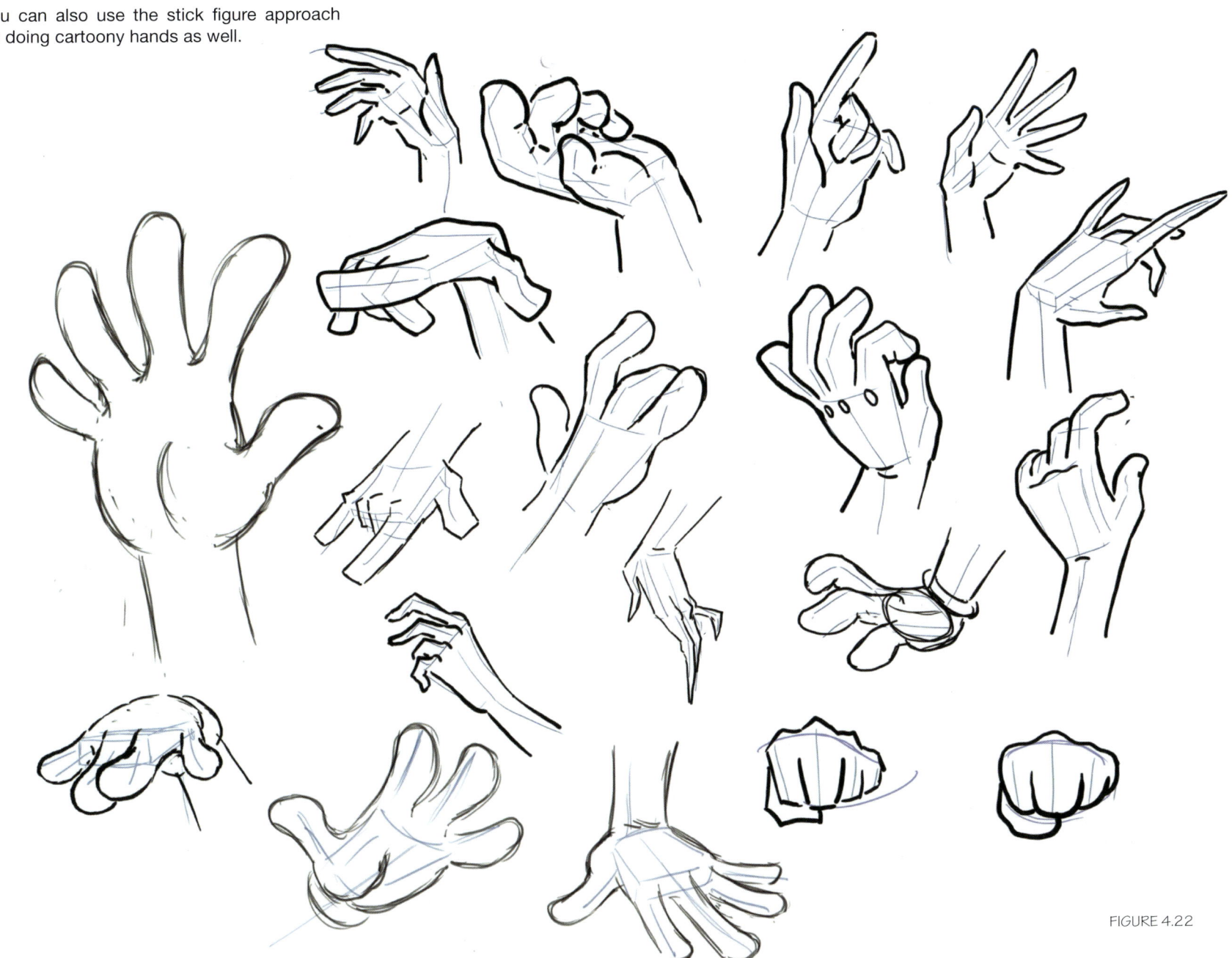

FIGURE 4.22

Claws, rings, bandages, nails all wrap or sit on the finger in a specific way. The nail sits right in the middle of the finger; the claw also sits in the middle of the finger and extends from the middle tip of the finger; the ring and bandage wrap around fingers as it would a tube.

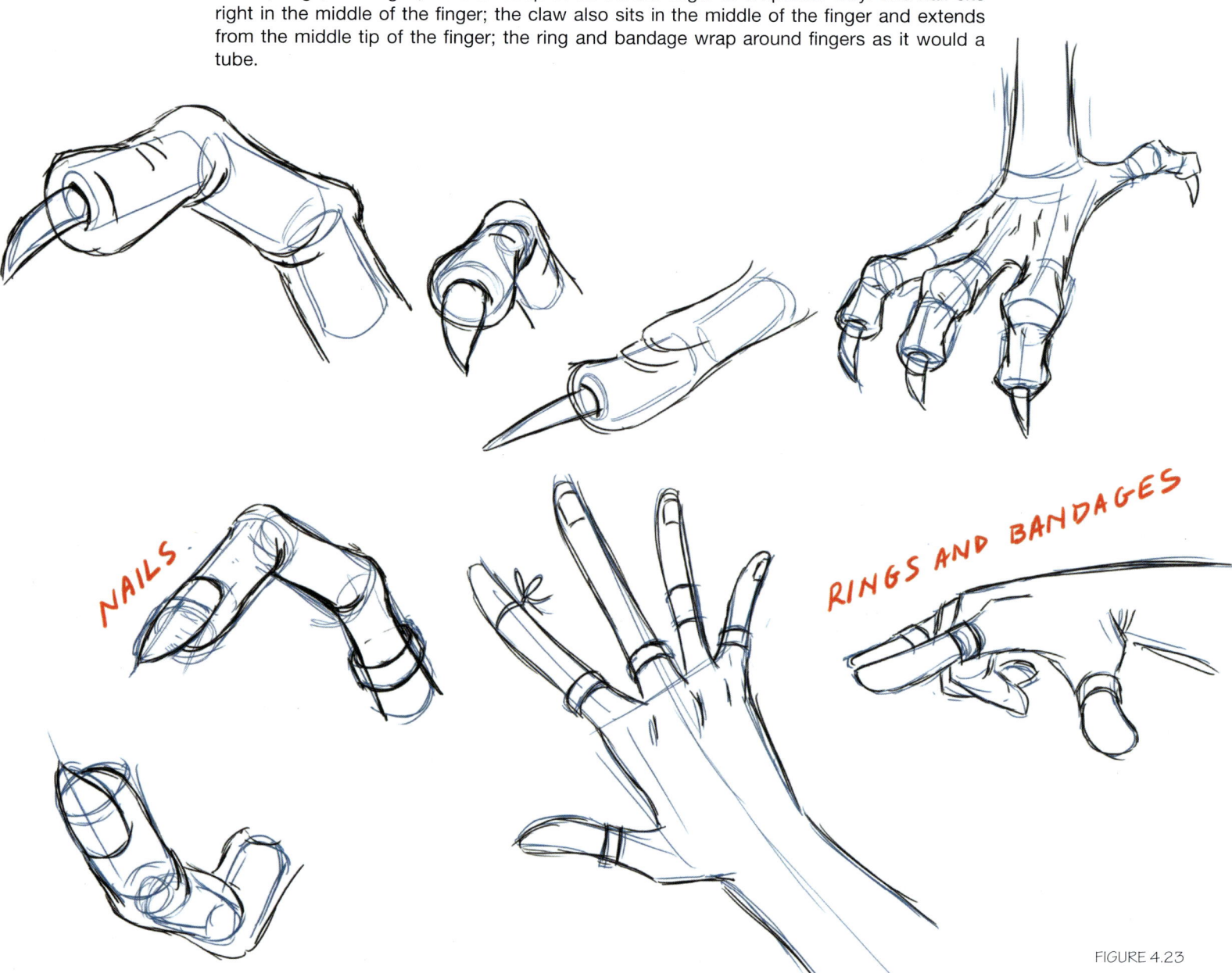

NAILS

RINGS AND BANDAGES

FIGURE 4.23

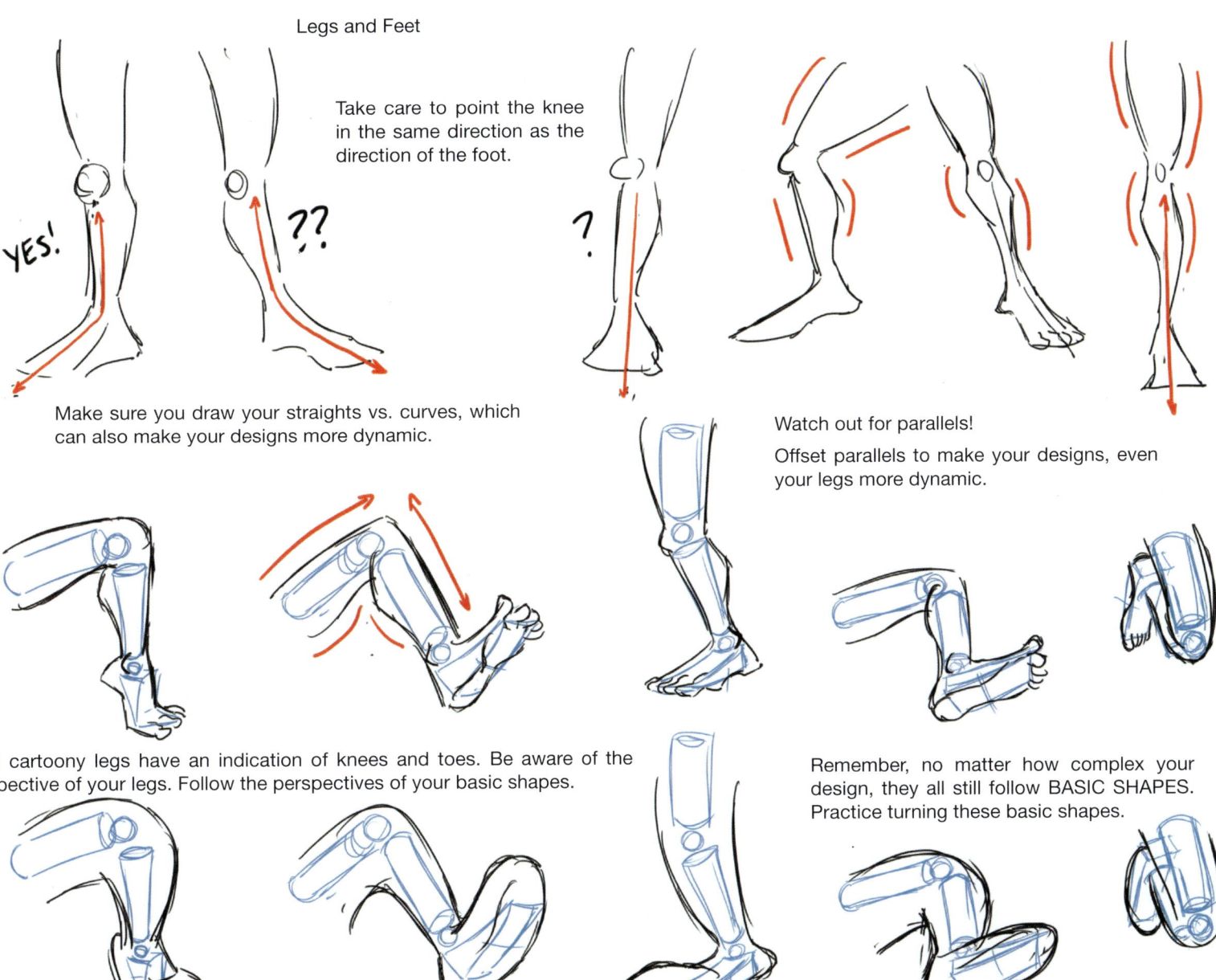

Legs and Feet

Take care to point the knee in the same direction as the direction of the foot.

YES!

??

?

Make sure you draw your straights vs. curves, which can also make your designs more dynamic.

Watch out for parallels!

Offset parallels to make your designs, even your legs more dynamic.

Even cartoony legs have an indication of knees and toes. Be aware of the perspective of your legs. Follow the perspectives of your basic shapes.

Remember, no matter how complex your design, they all still follow BASIC SHAPES. Practice turning these basic shapes.

FIGURE 4.24

The Foot

In general, the shoe heel sits in the middle of the bottom of the heel, so you can design anything you like as long as it falls directly below the heel.

If you draw a rectangular box of the shoe wedge first, you will be able to sort out the perspective of your shoes while still making super cool-looking shoes!

Stick that heel out from the shape of the wedge!

The heel of boots is like a squared off end of a box.

The shape of the sole of a flat shoe follows the base part of the upper section of the shoe. You can make the sole really thick or thin.

Make sure shoelaces cross through the center of the shoe.

Be sure to point the tip of the shoe right in the middle of the foot! It will clearly indicate the direction of the foot when you design your characters.

FIGURE 4.25

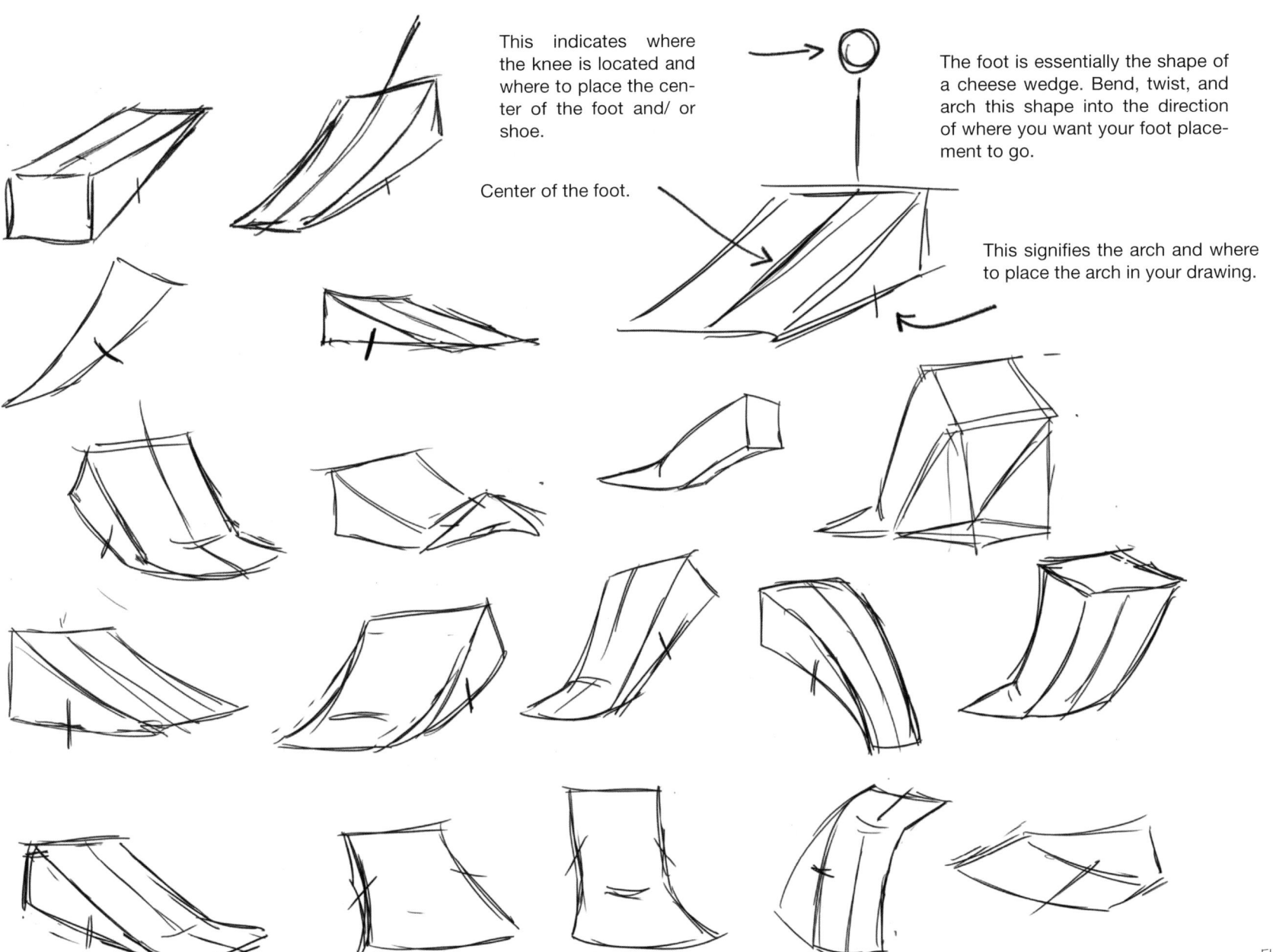

This indicates where the knee is located and where to place the center of the foot and/ or shoe.

Center of the foot.

The foot is essentially the shape of a cheese wedge. Bend, twist, and arch this shape into the direction of where you want your foot placement to go.

This signifies the arch and where to place the arch in your drawing.

FIGURE 4.26

Draw Space - Draw your ideas and sketches here!

It is best to push those toes off to the side, rather than draw them coming straight toward the viewer. It makes for a more appealing design of your character's feet.

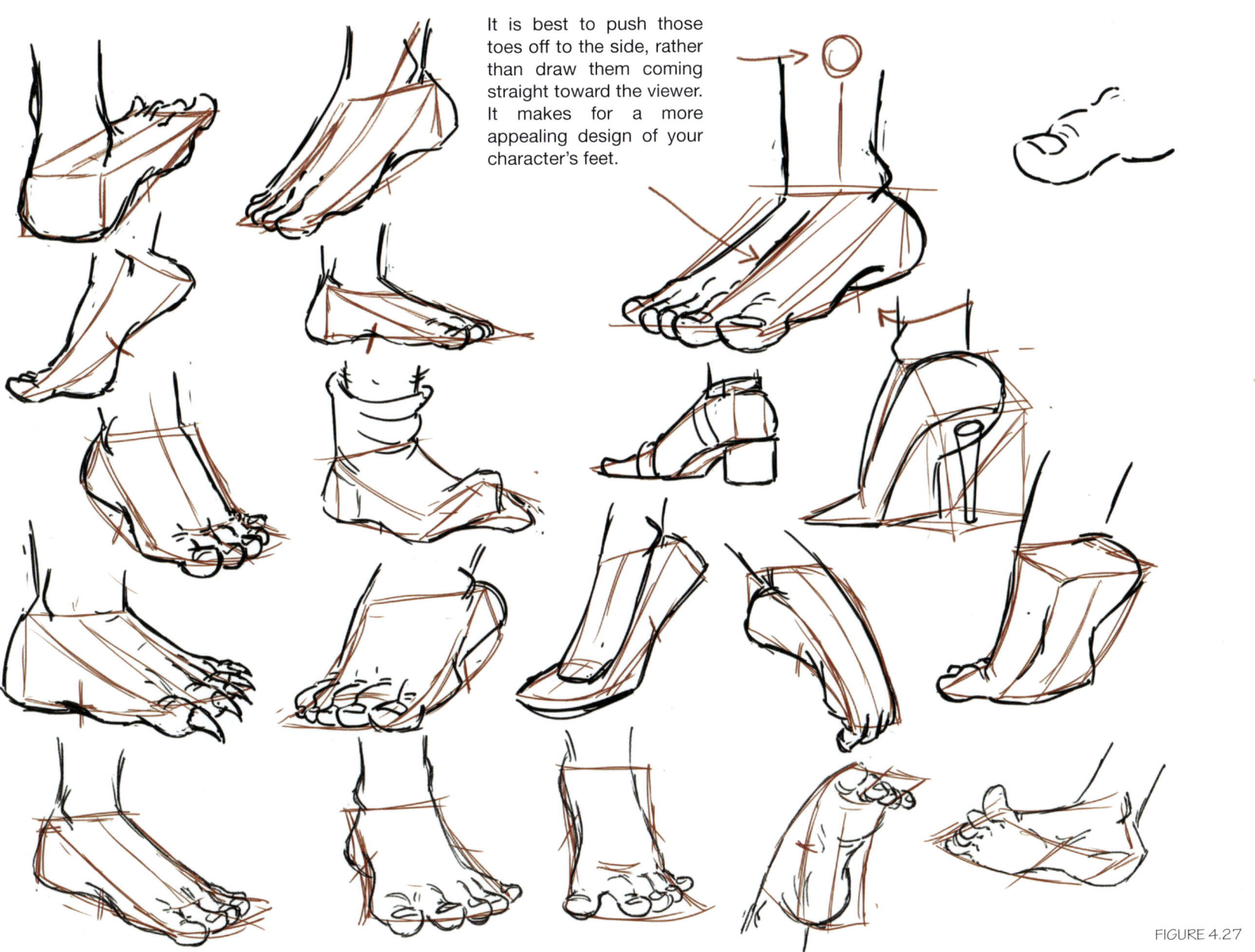

FIGURE 4.27

5

Ages

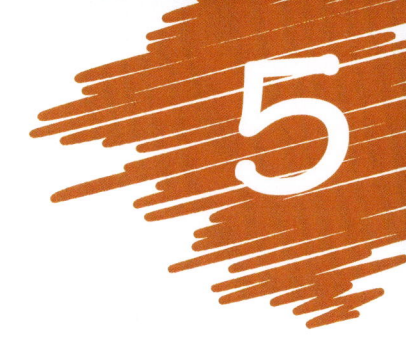

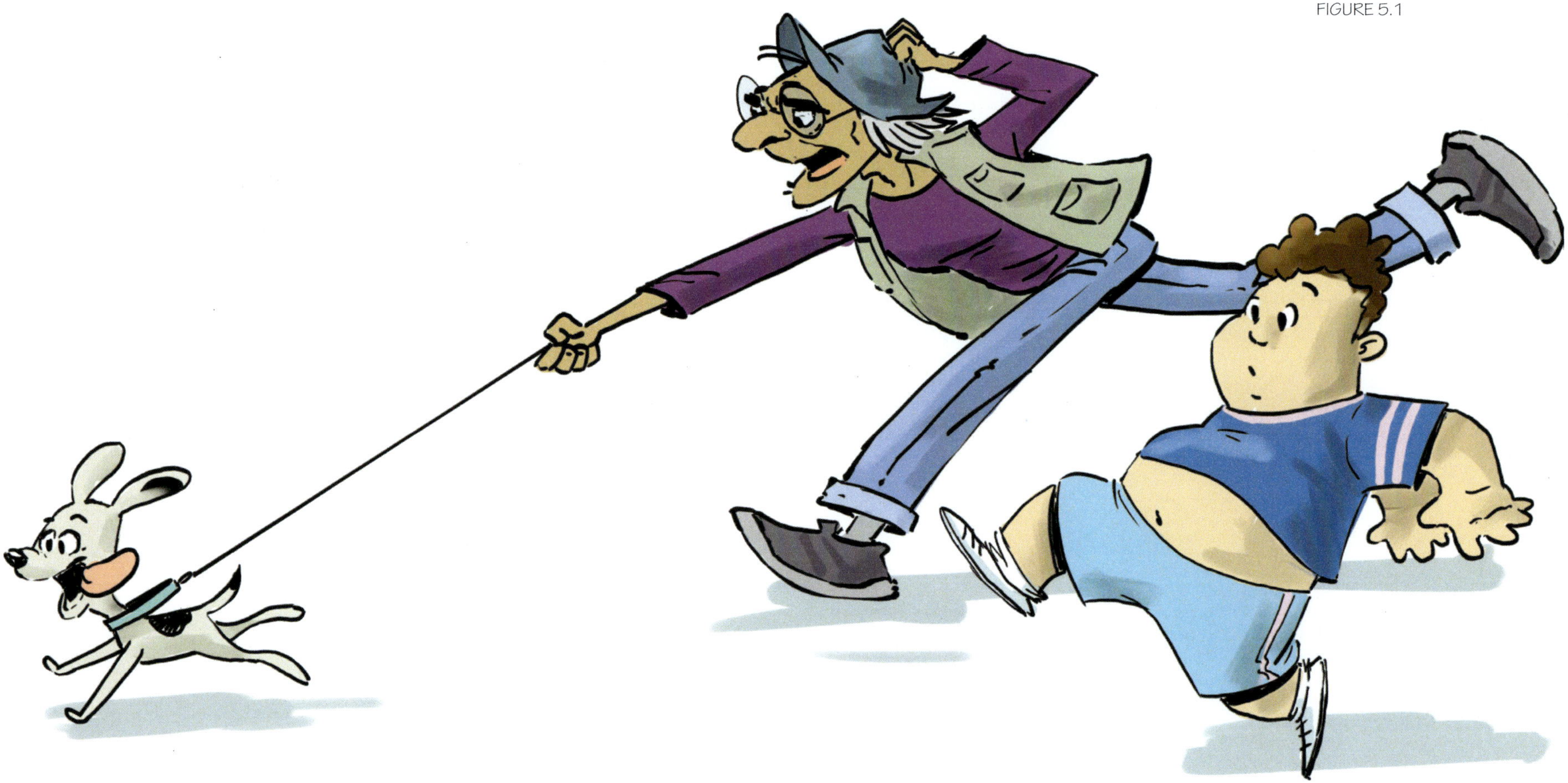

FIGURE 5.1

DOI: 10.1201/9781003599005-5

Ages

Humans come in all shapes and sizes, and there are so many societal factors that can influence the look of your character – war, famine, wealth, abundance – but humans all age in the same way. So let's take a look at what Mother Nature gives to us as we age! Be as accurate to the age of your character as possible. Be sure to be observant of the people around you and be inspired by what you see. Be sure to do your research. Everyone – male, female, and folks of other identities – experiences age similarly!

Keep the neck short when drawing toddlers…. It helps keep them looking really young!

Newborns and Infants: Newborns are children who typically are around 0–3 months old. Newborns typically cannot lift or turn their heads and – will need feeding about every 2 hours. Infants typically can lift their heads, can be portrayed as chunky and cute, and can roll over on their own after about 3 months old, which is a sign of the beginning of independent movement. Some infants are able to cruise and sometime even walk between 6 and 12 months. When designing newborns and infants, make sure to keep the muzzle small, round, and cute, as this area is still really unformed.

Newborns don't have baby fat just yet, as they are fresh out of the womb! They gain that baby fat from lots of food intake, which happens pretty quickly after birth. From there, you can draw the cute chunky baby!

Toddlers are typically under the age of 5, and still have baby fat but it less prominent because toddlers can walk, albeit clumsily. Keep the muzzle round and cute. Toddlers before the age of 3 are still in diapers and are typically messy, filthy. Toddlers are very curious, as they explore their new world and are incredibly imaginative.

FIGURE 5.2

Grade school kids between the ages of 7 and 11 are skinny and taller with little to no baby fat left, though it does vary between the individuals. You still want to keep the muzzle area small and the neck short, but you can add more definition to the face here. Kids around this age begin to become more self-aware and more assured on their feet.

Kids from the age of 10 to 12, pre-teens, become more self-conscious and self-aware at this age. This begins the onset of puberty. Females can be taller than males. You can begin to show the presence of breasts and slight hips but keep it to a minimum. Keep the muzzle soft but it is longer and has some definition in the face – You can lengthen the neck a tad more. Pre-teens' limbs are longer as Nature is beginning to push the young human to adult size. This is the beginning of "growing pains"!

Teenagers face full on puberty: raging hormones, the growth of hair at all different places of the body, breasts, limbs, ears, feet, hands, etc. Mental, physical, and emotional changes are happening during this critical growth stage. Take note: A lot of animated shows take place at this stage because of all these changes. Kids are finding their independence and direction in their lives. Here is where you can capitalize on these changes!

FIGURE 5.3

Young adults, around the college age, experience their first taste of independence. Young adults still have youth on their side, so keep the muzzle soft with no wrinkles and a slightly longer neck. Keep the body soft, but things like the breasts and musculature are more evident here. Humans grow into their physical peak at this age range. Think that many professional athletes rise into prominence at around this age range!

People in their 50s begin to experience a decline, such as menopause in women and a slower metabolism. When this begins, people begin to slow down though they are still active and are portrayed as grandparents as well. Facial features are more defined as the collagen in the face begins to go away and there is considerable calcification of bones, leading to the larger growth of bones, the sagging of flesh down the cheeks, eyes, nose, hence the presence of wrinkles. Also, the nose, chin, and ears continue to grow, so this is where the nose can begin to droop over the mouth… The chin also begins to jet downwards and outwards. The body begins to hunch forward and in women, hormones are no longer produced in the body as much due to menopause.

Humans in their 30s – this is the beginning of adults who have now established careers and are often portrayed as young parents. In the athletic world, humans are often at their physical prime. Females can also have wider hips, due to childbirth. In fact, women experience a multitude of changes after childbirth so this may influence your stories… One can add some lines to the face but keep it simple. Wrinkles start to become more prominent in middle age.

Facial features, such as wrinkles, can be more defined in humans in their 40s. Bodies can get thicker from calcification of bones, which can make a human look larger and wider. Humans are often portrayed here as parents to early teens.

FIGURE 5.4

At this age range of 80s–90s, one can design humans with a hunch back because of medical issues like osteoporosis or the weakening of bones… decades of walking can take a major toll on hips and knees, which can create a waddle… Decades of eating, chewing and drinking can cause gum recession, tooth decay and loss. One can really droop the forehead, add as many lines as possible everywhere on the face, even drop the nose over the mouth and droop the cheeks.

FIGURE 5.5

Humans in their 60s are considered past their prime, as the saying goes… For women, menopause has come and gone and metabolism has slowed down even more. This is another major milestone where the body does break down, and humans are even slower in movement. You can add a lot more definition to the face, even a slight hunch to the back.

The 70s–80s is where one can animate an individual's waddle, where hips and knees start to fail, thanks to decades of walking, running, etc. The use of canes and other walking aids become more prominent in character design. People can even lose body fat as appetites and digestive systems start to fail. The collagen in the face has largely gone away so one can see prominent sagging of the cheeks, forehead, and eyes. In the eyelids, you can even create the sad eye look because the collagen in the lids is gone, causing the lids to sag, creating the sad eye look. Even the eyebrows experience this similar effect, causing the eyebrows to look as if the individual is scowling.

Expression Sheets

DOI: 10.1201/9781003599005-6

FIGURE 6.1

Expression Sheets

Lord Funkelrod

Expression sheets are documents that show the character in different poses and expressions. One can draw the character in a full body or 3/4 body or just the head, depending on if the project is limited animation or fully animated. The more information you give to your crew, the better!

Here, we have our example, Lord Funkelrod. I still keep our character rather rough; as we're still in the visual development phase of character design. A lot can change, even in this phase! Once you start drawing your character in different angles and poses, the design can change to accommodate what you've drawn in your expressions.

So how to start? An expression must be clear, on model, and appealing.

A good way to start is the "STICK FIGURE" approach.

Let's start simply, with just the head... let's draw our STICK FIGURE approach and draw a character as "happy."

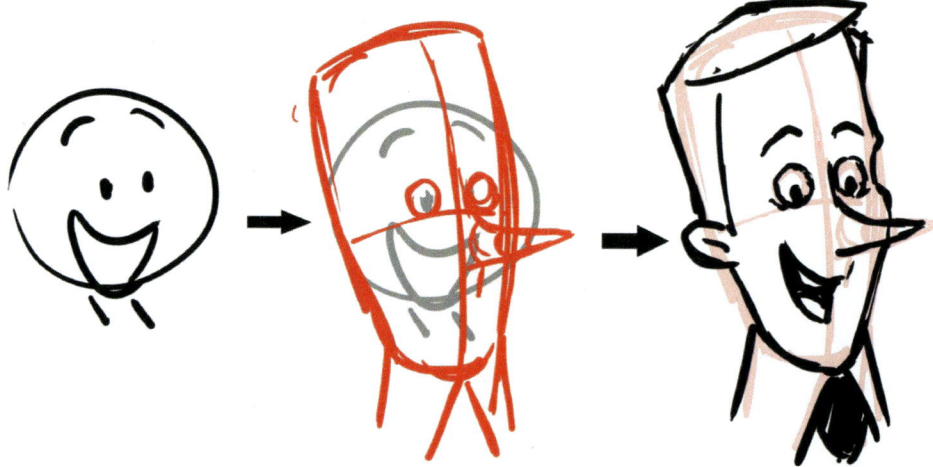

FIGURE 6.2

First, draw the head in the simplest of shapes. Add the cross hairs to make sure you line up the eyes, ears, and nose accurately. Also be sure to draw through your shapes, or else your character can potentially look disconnected in certain areas!

Break down your initial design into simple shapes: the tube, ball, cone, and cube. Once you break down into those shapes, draw your stick figure gesture. Remember to draw that line of action!

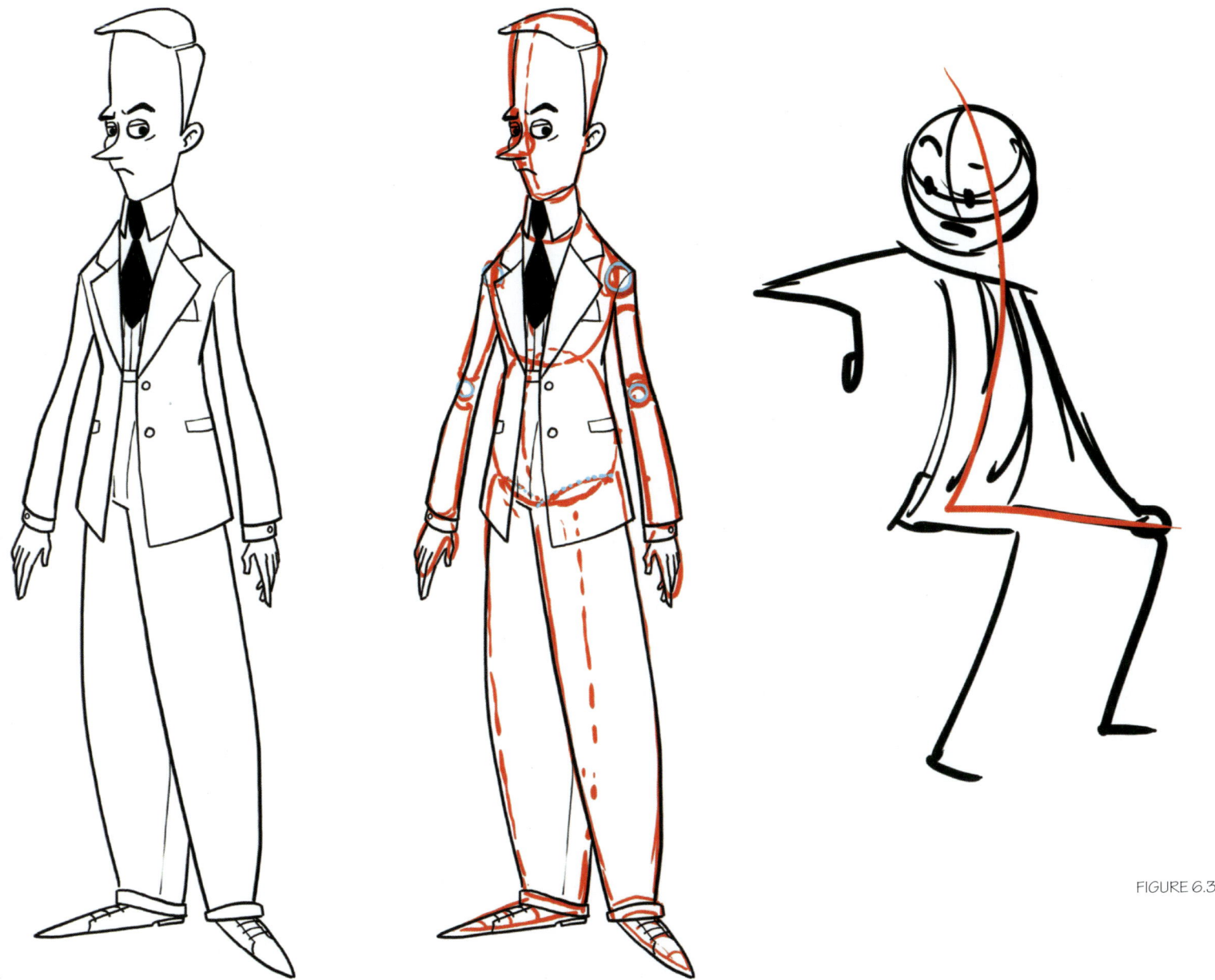

FIGURE 6.3

Draw Space - Draw your ideas and sketches here!

Now put those shapes in perspective, with the idea of putting those shapes in proportion to your character. Remember, the horizon line is typically at the eye line. I like to draw the floor plane, so I know how to plant those feet as well as the plane on which he sits, to show weight.

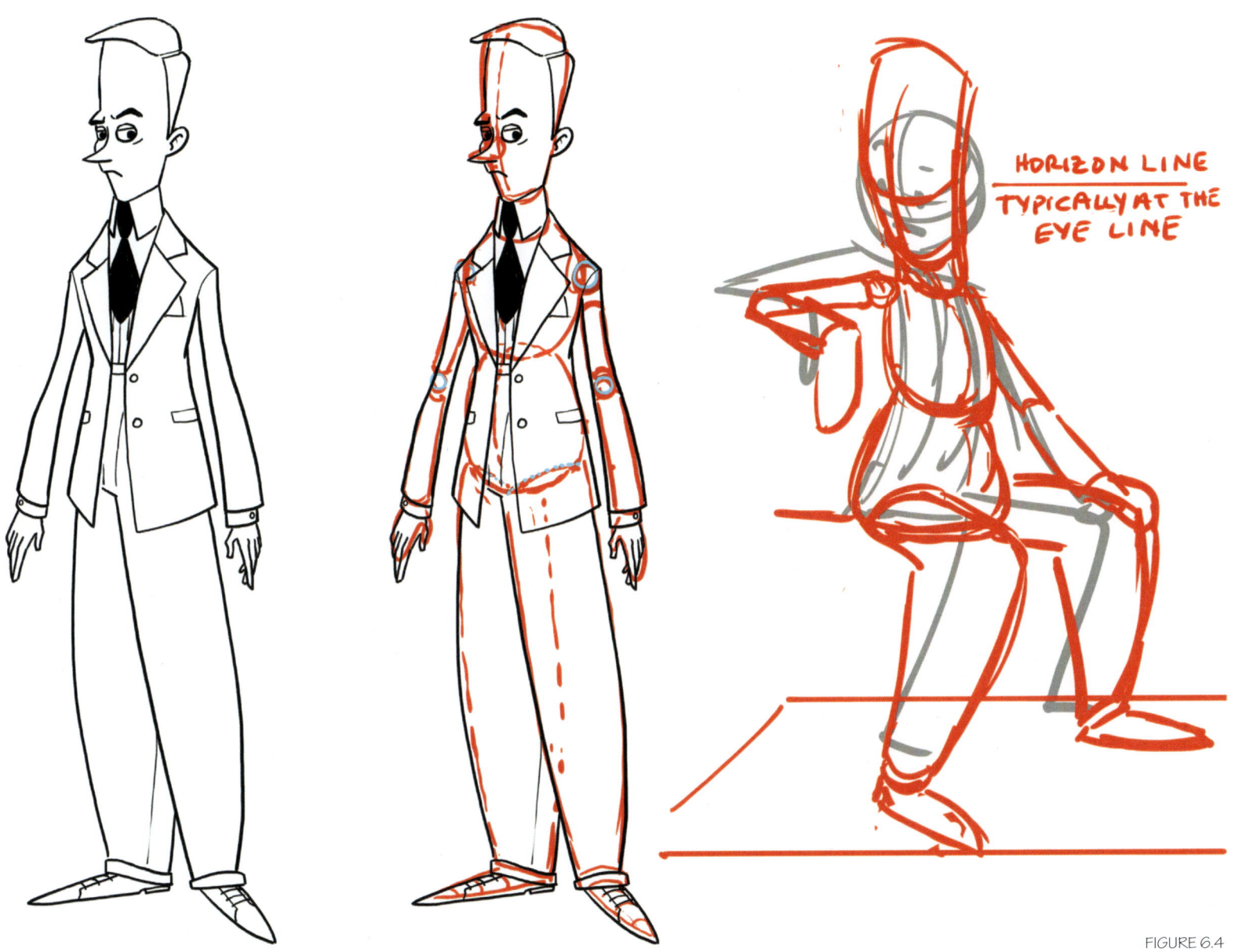

HORIZON LINE
TYPICALLY AT THE
EYE LINE

FIGURE 6.4

Draw Space - Draw your ideas and sketches here!

Now try to rough in the character to match the original model you have drawn. Make sure you avoid tangents, and center the tie, the vest and even the pants zipper, all of which run down the center of the body and will help show perspective.

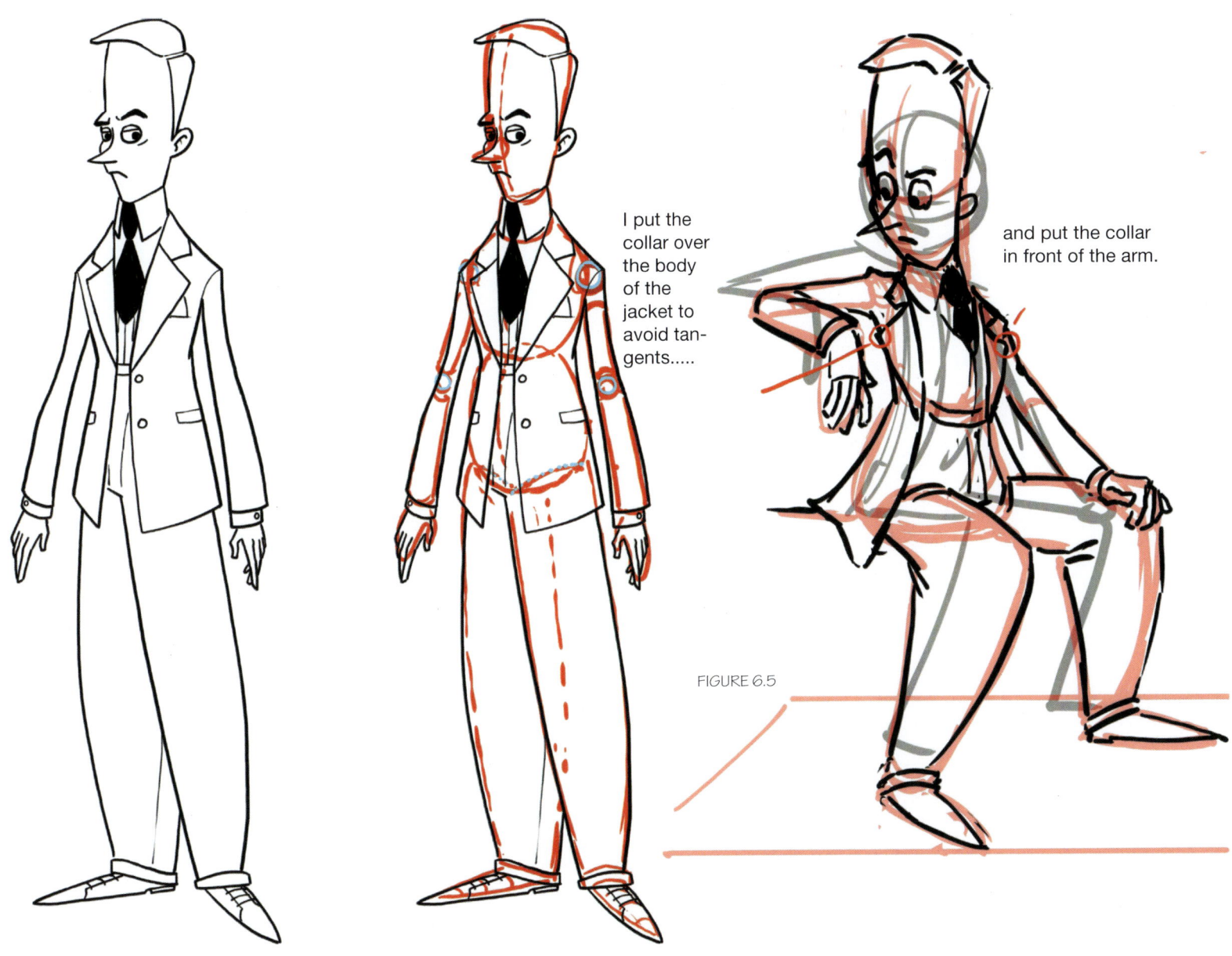

I put the collar over the body of the jacket to avoid tangents.....

and put the collar in front of the arm.

FIGURE 6.5

Draw Space - Draw your ideas and sketches here!

Lord Funkelrod

I'll take our hero drawing of Lord Funkelrod and keep him on our page. Then we use the STICK FIGURE drawing approach and draw some expressions. We take into account, the Line of Action, Clarity, and the unique way our Lord Funkelrod expresses himself.

FIGURE 6.6

Draw Space - Draw your ideas and sketches here!

Lord Funkelrod

Using these stick figure expressions, you can draw over each one, making sure you're on model at the same time, achieving clarity in your expression.

FIGURE 6.7

Draw Space - Draw your ideas and sketches here!

FIGURE 6.8

Here is another example of how to do expression sheets. As long as you have an idea of who your character is, you can create stick figures to draw whatever expression you like. Make sure that these stick figures are clear, even in this simplistic form.

Draw Space - Draw your ideas and sketches here!

When you draw your character in these expressions, you can use the stick figures as a guideline and make sure it's all clear and readable and, of course, on model.

FIGURE 6.9

Draw Space - Draw your ideas and sketches here!

FIGURE 6.10

This "stick figure" approach can be applied to any character you design. Just make sure your stick figure poses are clear in their expressions! Once you're satisfied with them, you can proceed to... (Flip to the next page to see!)

Remember, your Line of Action must be clear!

Draw Space - Draw your ideas and sketches here!

These red boxes represent the perspective plane upon which your character sits or stands. It is a good idea to add that plane at your character's feet, so you can draw those feet and ultimately, your character, solidly only that plane.

A fox...

A lady...

A sailor...

FIGURE 6.11

Clothing—Using Research, Reference, and Inspiration

FIGURE 7.1

DOI: 10.1201/9781003599005-7

Clothing—Using Research, Reference, and Inspiration

You know that saying, "Clothes makes the man"? Well, this applies to clothing your character. Clothing reflects a character's personality, their likes and dislikes, their attitudes, and their environment. For example, anyone can design a business person, but to truly get to design a cool business person is to know where that person is from, what kind of business this person is in, where this person lives and what is going on in that community/environment... All this and more can influence what this person can wear.

Like, what does a snake oil salesman from the 1800s western United States look like? Or a 1980s American, big city businesswoman look like?

Clark Stanley, who sold an herbal concoction across the western states in the late 1800s. His antics throughout the West coined the term snake oil salesman, in reference to the concoctions sold to gullible victims. Research can be found in what men wore around that time, in particular people who lived across the Wild West.

In the 1980s, business attire for women began to look like a feminine version of men's suits. Shoulder pads were big and in, as was big hair. And with the increase of corporate female workers, also came practicality: Women often wore sneakers to get to work, carrying their heels with their bags.

FIGURE 7.2

While you're doing research and reference, look at design styles. Look into illustrations, paintings... I look at children's books to discover different design styles that may influence how my characters will look. A great approach is to find great illustrators who may be of great influence to how you draw! Some of my favorites are Dan Santat, Wallace Tripp, the Provensens, and I also love Peter de Seve, J.C. Leyendecker, Terryl Whitlatch, and the painter, J.S. Sargent.

Design styles can come from styles that defined an era or a culture, for example: Art Deco, Medieval, cave art, and calligraphy. These types of styles can be very influential to design. Take, for example, The *Secret of Kells*, which was heavily influenced by Medieval Art and the art in the *Book of Kells*, which is heavy in Celtic design.

Once you have found some design styles that inspire you, try designing characters in different styles. As a designer, you must be able to find the visual cues that make up that particular design style and incorporate them into your design.

For example, if the design style is Art Deco, take a look at great artists like Erte, Tamara de Lempicka, and ask yourself, what are the visual cues that define Art Deco?

FIGURE 7.3

The key to making an authentically designed character is doing deep, meaningful research. It will give your character integrity and truthfulness and less chance of stereotyping.

Helpful hint: GO TO THE LIBRARY! The library is an incredible resource for digging deep into your character's world, different and little known facts that can inform your character. It is okay to scour the internet for information, of course – but it's beneficial to go to the library to discover things about your character that will bring honor and integrity to your designs.

REFERENCE and RESEARCH refer to finding work within factual history. Even if you are working on a fantastical story, your costume designs can still come from a place and time that exists in our lifetime. For example, the fantasy show, Blue Eye Samurai takes place during the era when the English traded with Japan in the Edo period. Much of the costume design reflects this.

You can also find INSPIRATION anywhere! Inspiration can be found in films, show, picture books, fashion, and music. For example, the live action film *Pirates of the Caribbean* character Jack Sparrow is influenced by the looks of rock and roll, specifically, Keith Richards of the Rolling Stones. So while parts of this character are based on some element of real and true pirates of legend, other parts are inspired by rock music.

You can mix and match research, reference, and inspiration and create something amazing! The most successful character designs are an amalgam of all these three elements of character development.

FIGURE 7.4

This is a small example of research on fashion in the 80s, to inform clothing designs for my character designs. It is crucial to take a deep dive into your characters' world and culture to create the best clothing design that will reflect your character's personality, mood, and situation.

Here's an example of some characters I designed and researched from what was hot and popular during the 1980s. One character was inspired by the big British music scene that invaded the United States during the 1980s, specifically, Culture Club and the rise of androgyny in pop music, Duran Duran and Madonna. At the same time, the preppy look came into prominence, with fashion designers like Ralph Lauren, Gloria Vanderbilt, and Calvin Klein rose to fame with polo shirts, designer jeans, and K Swiss. So, we have a mish-mash of high school students, ranging from Mods, geeks and nerds, preppies, and fan girls… It was a great time…

Doing research can be a lot of fun! It can be fascinating to look at not just pop culture, but also the events that were happening during the time period you are researching. Oftentimes, music and pop culture are a reflection of what is happening politically and socioeconomically. Take that deep dive and discover what you can find!

It is crucial to research into your characters' world and culture to create the best clothing design that will reflect your character's personality, mood, and situation.

Design Styles

FIGURE 8.1

DOI: 10.1201/9781003599005-8

Design Styles

Research and reference is really useful for developing a unique style for your designs. It's important to look for the visual cues that are specific to that style and then use those cues to incorporate them into your own drawings.

Challenge yourself by drawing your characters in different design styles, based on the research and reference you can find. Try to make them as distinct as possible and look for visual cues in the reference so that your design can closely resemble that style!

Take note that even your rendering can be different in each style...

FIGURE 8.2
ADOBESTOCK_383462794

FIGURE 8.3
ADOBESTOCK_383464809

FIGURE 8.4

FIGURE 8.5
ADOBESTOCK_478942028

I usually start here, with the style I am familiar with and draw often... cartoony and cute.

I love the way the Japanese artists painted tigers during the 18th century – unusual, stylized, and ultimately interesting and unique.

FIGURE 8.6
DP-17989-073

FIGURE 8.8

FIGURE 8.7
DP-31478-005

FIGURE 8.9
DP232503

This design style is inspired by the beautiful work in the book – *My Father's Dragon*.

FIGURE 8.10

FIGURE 8.11

This style reflects the work discovered in the Art Deco style, my favorite designer, the incredible Erte.

FIGURE 8.12

FIGURE 8.13

9

Animals

FIGURE 9.1

DOI: 10.1201/9781003599005-9

Horses and Other Four-Legged Herbivores

Horses, like all other herbivorous animals, are shaped similarly in terms of how the legs move and where the musculature is placed. Remember to locate familiar body parts on the horse, as they move similarly to the human. For example, the horse has a scapula, wrists, knees, elbows, etc., just like a human. It's just a matter of locating them.

Also, some fun facts are that horses, like most other herbivores, have eyes on the side of their head because they are often on the lookout for predators. And they walk on a nail. Other herbivorous animals, such as deer and antelope, walk on two or three nails.

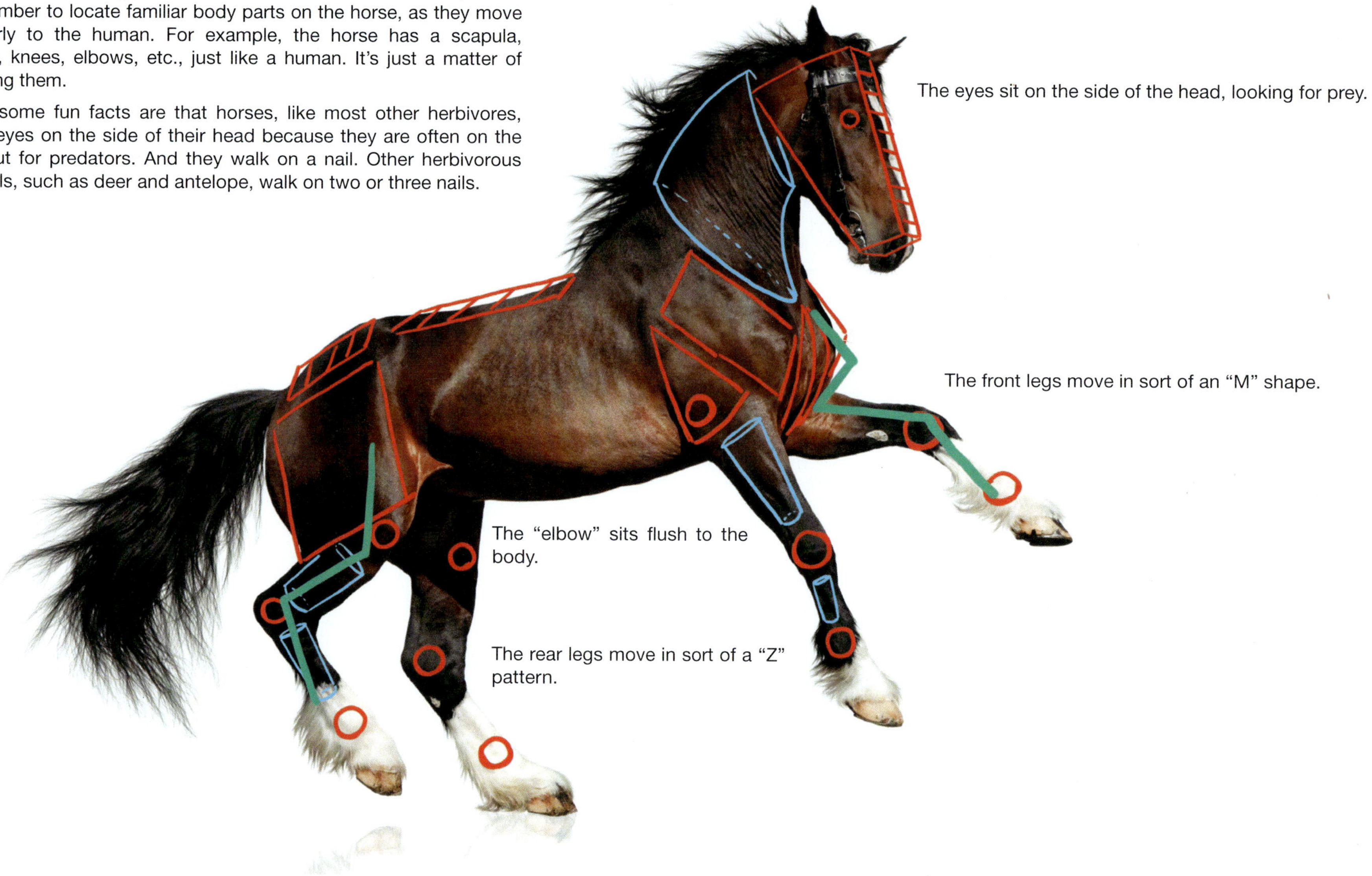

The eyes sit on the side of the head, looking for prey.

The front legs move in sort of an "M" shape.

The "elbow" sits flush to the body.

The rear legs move in sort of a "Z" pattern.

FIGURE 9.2
(REFERENCE: ADOBESTOCK_38247523)

Break the body and musculature into basic shapes: tubes, boxes, balls, and pyramids. Once you get it, you can caricature...

"M" SHAPE

"Z" SHAPE

FIGURE 9.3
(REFERENCE: ADOBESTOCK_38247523)

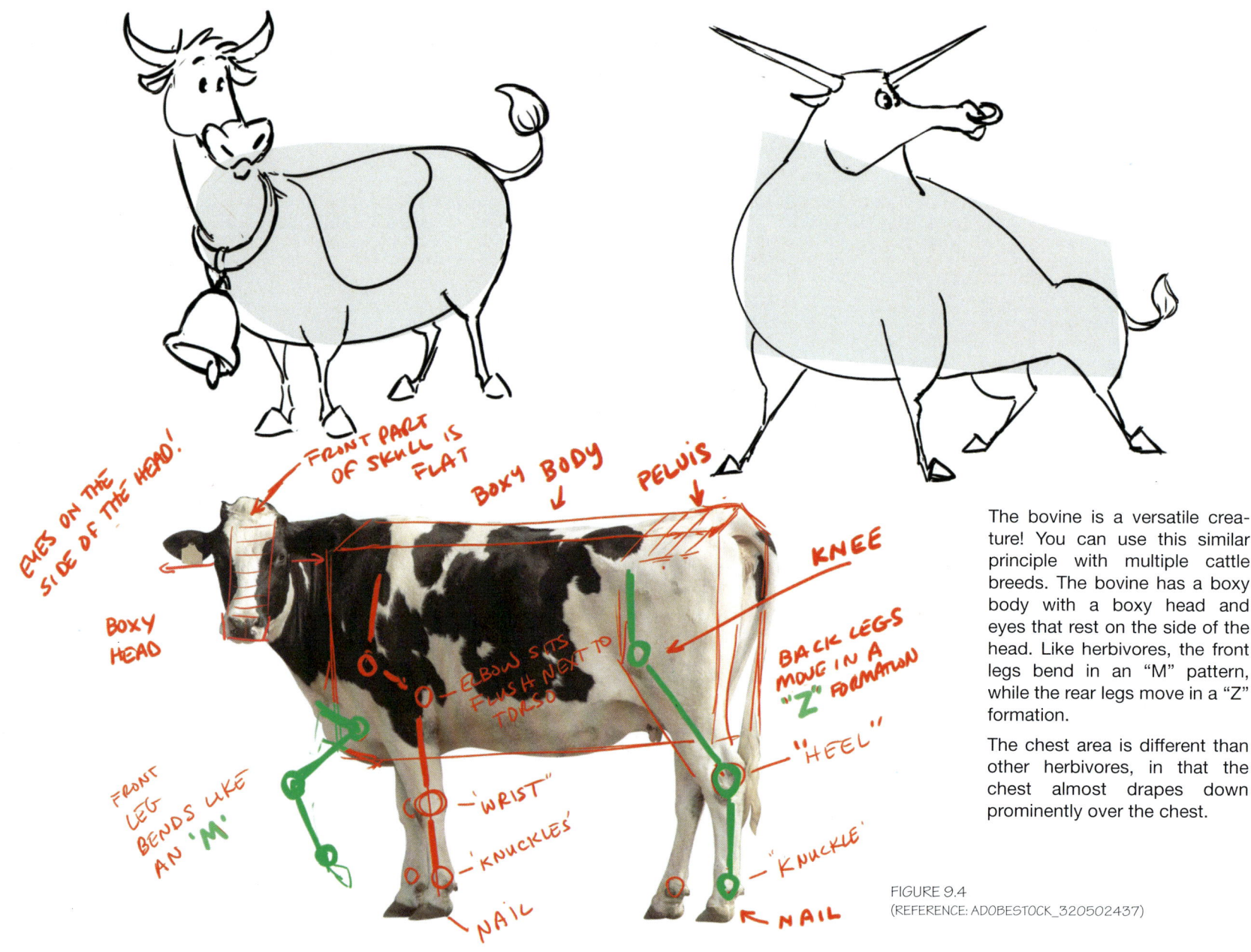

EYES ON THE SIDE OF THE HEAD!

FRONT PART OF SKULL IS FLAT

BOXY BODY

PELVIS

KNEE

BOXY HEAD

O-ELBOW SITS FLUSH NEXT TO TORSO

BACK LEGS MOVE IN A "Z" FORMATION

"HEEL"

FRONT LEG BENDS LIKE AN 'M'

O-'WRIST'

O-'KNUCKLES'

O-"KNUCKLE

NAIL

NAIL

The bovine is a versatile creature! You can use this similar principle with multiple cattle breeds. The bovine has a boxy body with a boxy head and eyes that rest on the side of the head. Like herbivores, the front legs bend in an "M" pattern, while the rear legs move in a "Z" formation.

The chest area is different than other herbivores, in that the chest almost drapes down prominently over the chest.

FIGURE 9.4
(REFERENCE: ADOBESTOCK_320502437)

DEER or animals of a similar build, such as the antelope, goat, etc., have boxy bodies and powerful legs. Deer are incredibly large and agile animals, built to leap powerfully in zig-zagging motions to avoid prey.

I use the same approach to animals of similar build and shape, like goats, antelope, and gazelle.

EYES ON SIDE OF HEAD

NECK IS A TUBE

PECTORALS

SHOULDER

ELBOW

"WRIST"

'KNUCKLE'

NAILS

✓ BOXY BODY

KNEE

'HEEL'

'KNUCKLE'

YA GOT A PROBLEM WITH DAT?

FIGURE 9.5
(REFERENCE: ADOBESTOCK_225436863)

Like most herbivores, the front legs move in an "M" pattern and the rear legs move in a "Z" pattern.

Rodents

Rodents can include rabbits, guinea pigs, beavers, squirrels, hamsters, rats... The anatomy is similar!

I did this one to demonstrate that it doesn't capture mouse-like characteristics very well and doesn't work. No matter how cartoony or how realistic you are, you must demonstrate clearly that it looks like a mouse.

What makes a mouse look like a mouse? Again, you want to capture the essence and specific characteristics of a mouse... and then go nuts and have fun!

An easy fix is to increase the ear size and tail... done!

FIGURE 9.6
(REFERENCE: ADOBESTOCK_243630551)

FIGURE 9.9
(REFERENCE: ADOBESTOCK_25316955)

Rabbits possess a similar anatomy structure as rats, mice, and guinea pigs: they are all rodents, after all! Note the head is egg shaped, but in the world of cartoons, you are capturing the essence of what makes a rabbit a rabbit: the teeth, the ears, the feet, and the cheeky muzzle....

FIGURE 9.7

FIGURE 9.8
(REFERENCE: ADOBESTOCK_535924732)

EVEN US WEREWOLVES COME FROM CANINES!

Canines

Canines, such as wolves and domesticated dogs, are predatory creatures: wolves, as wild animals, carry their heads down in a crouched position, as if always in a hunt, while most domesticated dogs keep their heads more upright. Wild dogs are generally leaner and meaner in stature and physicality.

The muzzle, in general, is more boxy than on felines.

Front legs and rear legs move in a "Z" pattern

SHOULDERS
CHEST
ELBOWS
WRIST
KNEES
HEELS

SHOULDER
"WRIST"
CANINES WALK ON TOES
ELBOW
KNEE
SHIN
HEEL

FIGURE 9.10
(REFERENCE: ADOBESTOCK_132891893, ADOBESTOCK_372050465, ADOBESTOCK_372050465)

FELINES are sophisticated predators! They have incredible flexibility, so much so that they can land from great heights and take down running prey as it zig zags across the plains, and it is this flexibility that allows a feline to hang on till the deed is done. They can leap at great heights to capture flying prey, using their paws to grasp and take down. Their tails are not just communication tools; they are also useful in balancing the feline as they leap, jump, and run. Indeed, the feline species is an efficient and great animal.

As a predator, they are similarly structured to canines, in that the wrist area is low on the forearms... This kind of anatomy makes it easy to caricature the feline! The trick is to recognize and look through the fluff and fur so you can successfully illustrate your feline.

Felines fight and kill with their teeth, feet, and front paws, compared to canines, which mostly fight and kill with their powerful jaws and teeth and sometimes their front paws.

FIGURE 9.11
(REFERENCE:
ADOBESTOCK_79253230,
ADOBESTOCK_310909442,
ADOBESTOCK_79253230)

Understanding how limbs and legs work similarly to humans will help you draw difficult poses like this one. You can draw perspectives in areas such as the arms if you know that they are tubes and boxes, and can draw those tubes and boxes in perspective!

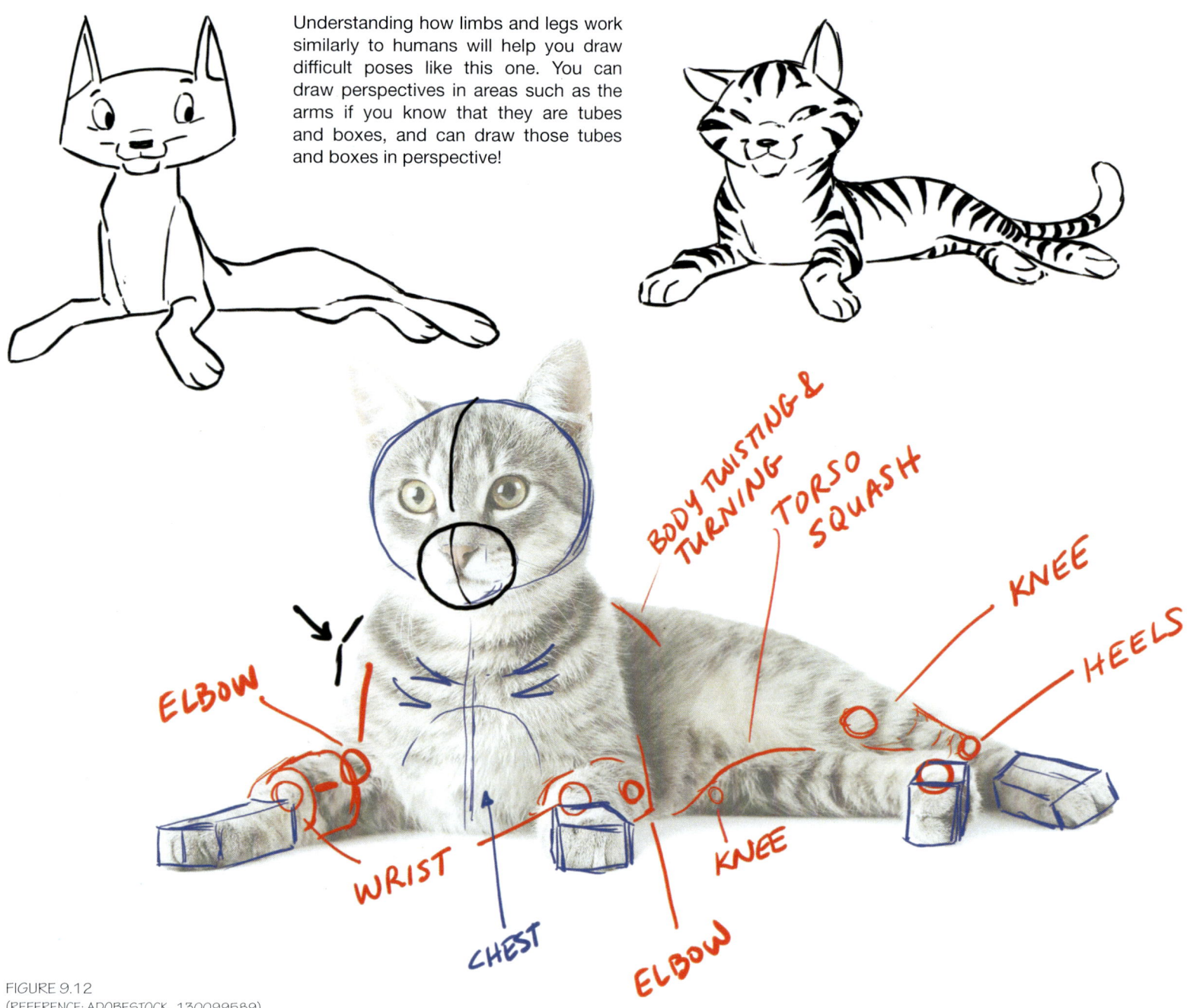

FIGURE 9.12
(REFERENCE: ADOBESTOCK_130099589)

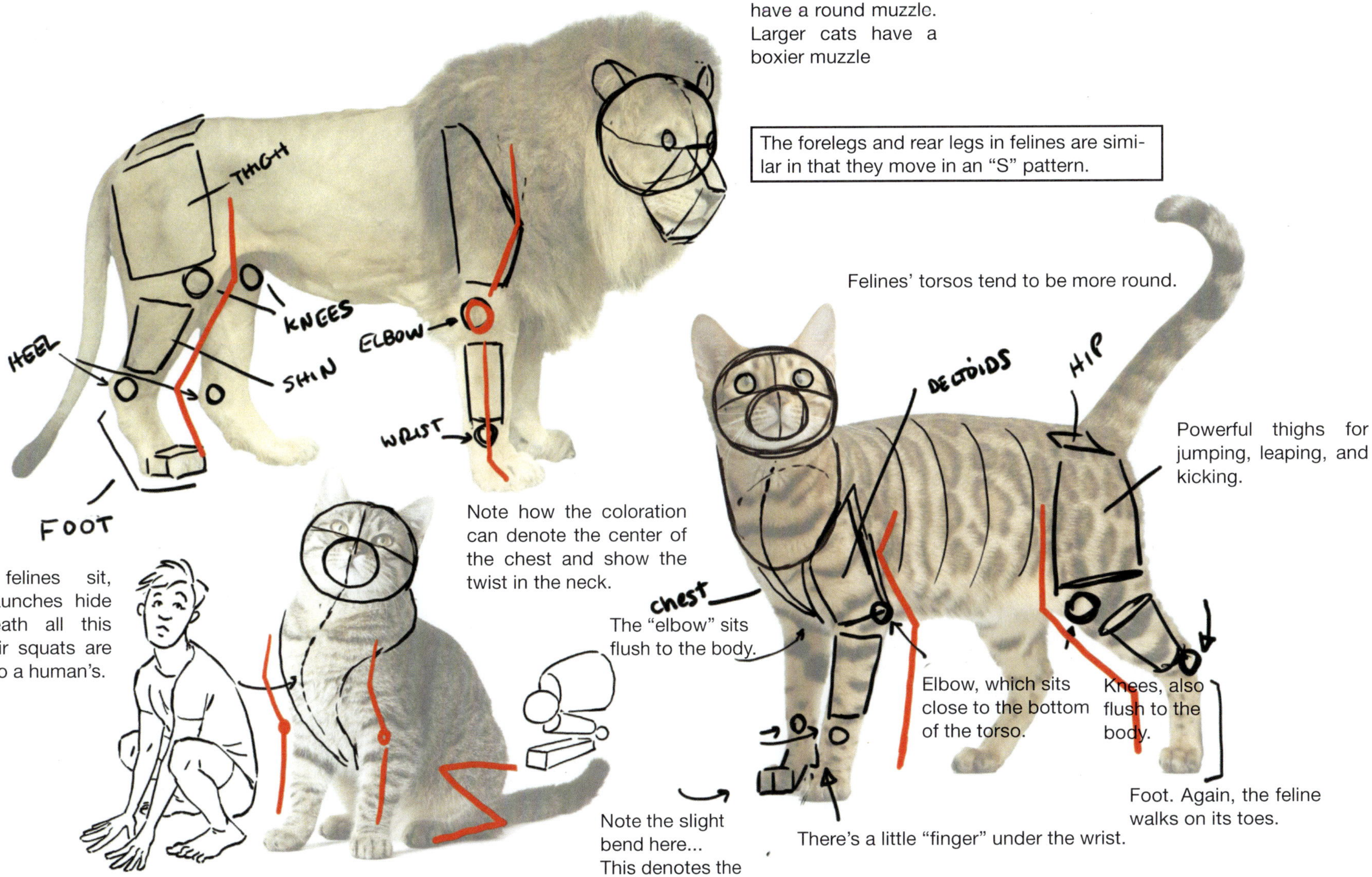

Like all predators, the eyes face forward on the skull, because the predator is always looking directly at their prey during a chase!

FIGURE 9.13
(REFERENCE: ADOBESTOCK_79253230, ADOBESTOCK_310909442, ADOBESTOCK_79253230)

Domestic cats can have a round muzzle. Larger cats have a boxier muzzle

The forelegs and rear legs in felines are similar in that they move in an "S" pattern.

THIGH

KNEES

ELBOW

HEEL

SHIN

WRIST

FOOT

Felines' torsos tend to be more round.

DELTOIDS

HIP

Powerful thighs for jumping, leaping, and kicking.

chest

When felines sit, their haunches hide underneath all this fur. Their squats are similar to a human's.

Note how the coloration can denote the center of the chest and show the twist in the neck.

The "elbow" sits flush to the body.

Elbow, which sits close to the bottom of the torso.

Knees, also flush to the body.

Foot. Again, the feline walks on its toes.

Note the slight bend here... This denotes the "wrist."

Felines walk on their toes.

There's a little "finger" under the wrist.

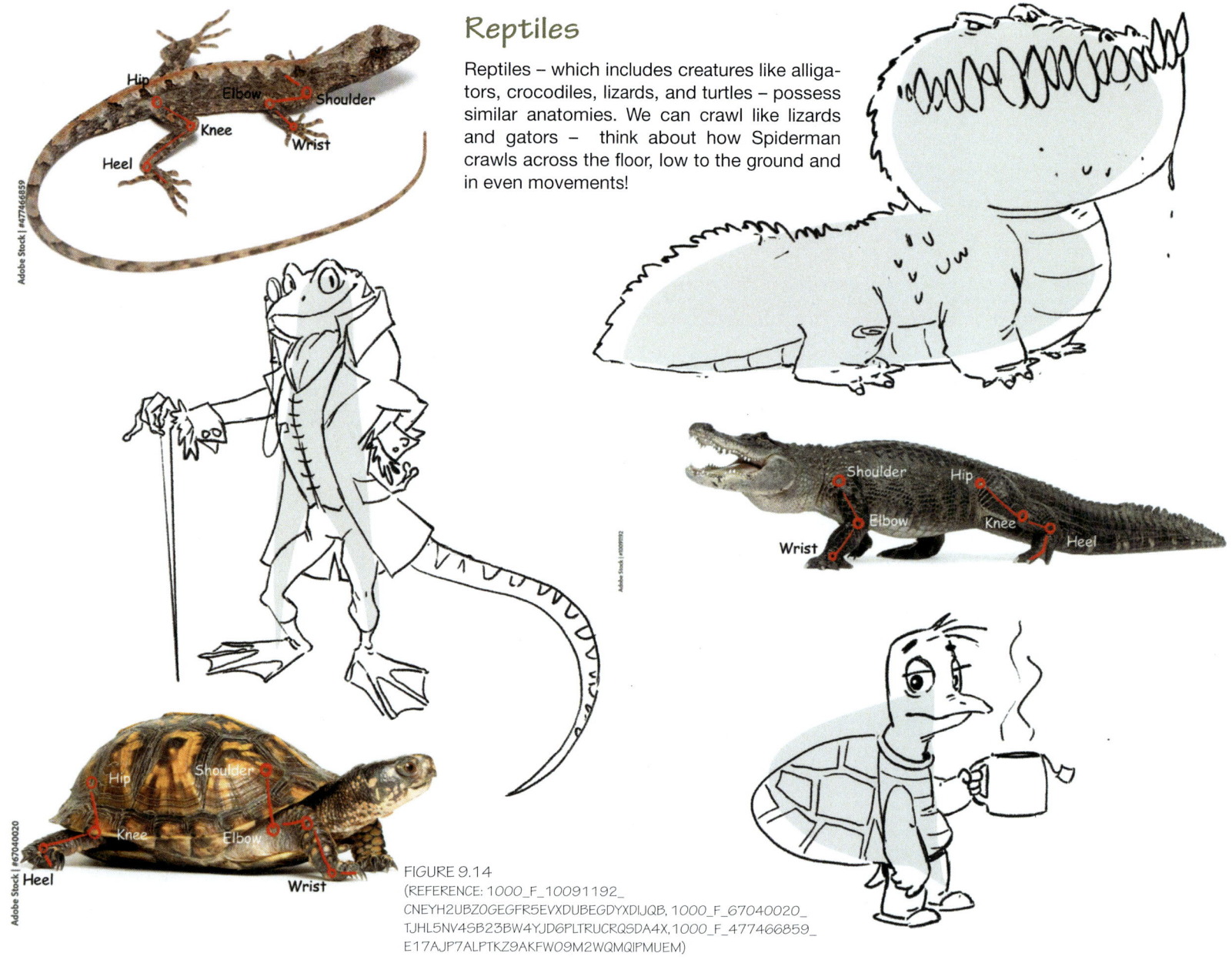

Reptiles

Reptiles – which includes creatures like alligators, crocodiles, lizards, and turtles – possess similar anatomies. We can crawl like lizards and gators – think about how Spiderman crawls across the floor, low to the ground and in even movements!

FIGURE 9.14
(REFERENCE: 1000_F_10091192_
CNEYH2UBZ0GEGFR5EVXDUBEGDYXDIJQB, 1000_F_67040020_
TJHL5NV4SB23BW4YJD6PLTRUCRQSDA4X, 1000_F_477466859_
E17AJP7ALPTKZ9AKFWO9M2WQMQIPMUEM)

Birds

Birds have a round aerodynamic body full of feathers, so the thighs, knees, and shins (otherwise known as the drumstick) are all hidden in a backwards "Z" configuration underneath this feathery body. What you see is just the feet. What you see in the curvature of the wings are the "wrists" and "fingers" that extend down into the wings.

You can design this small bird any way you want... realistically, super cartoony, simplified, as long as you capture the ESSENCE and key characteristics of this particular bird.

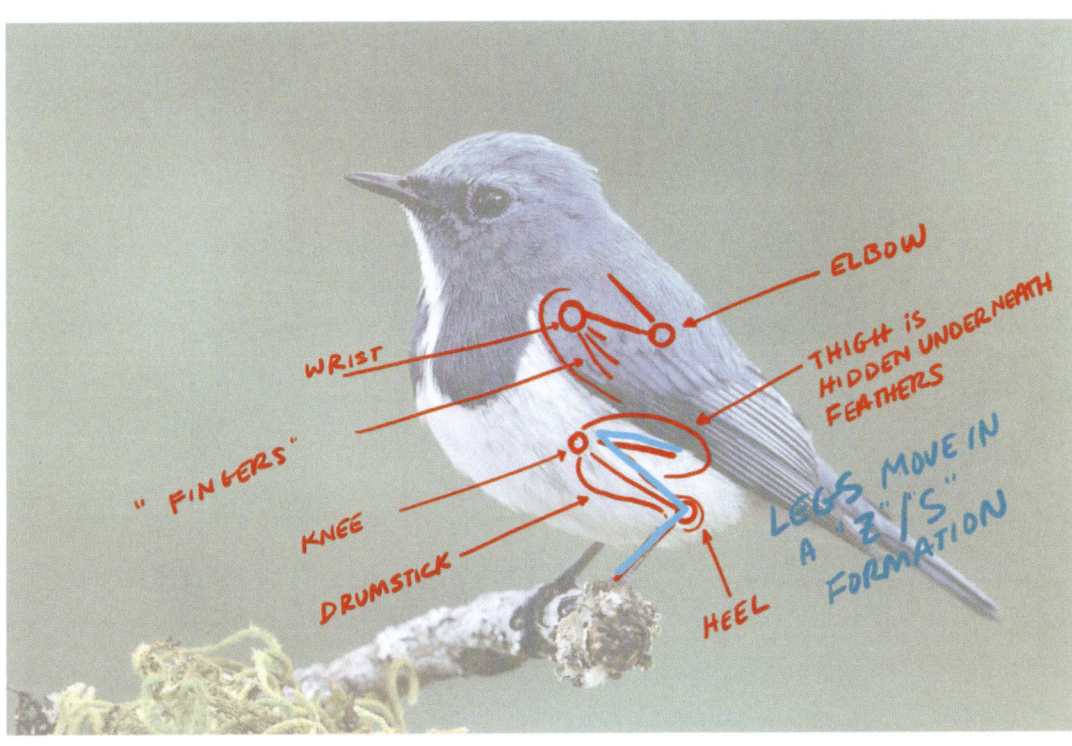

FIGURE 9.15
(REFERENCE: ADOBESTOCK_177476718)

FIGURE 9.16
(REFERENCE: ADOBESTOCK_202927518, ADOBESTOCK_394838459)

Predatory Birds

Predatory birds, such as owls, hawks, and eagles, have a few similarities, like massive claws. They are larger than those of smaller birds, which hunt smaller prey like worms and bugs. Large birds use their large legs and claws to tear, grab, carry and crush their prey. Most predatory birds have eyes that face forward as it provides focus on the hunt. And they are BIG, with some having wing spans of over 6 feet wide. Beaks are sharp, used for tearing.

Turnarounds

FIGURE 10.1

DOI: 10.1201/9781003599005-10

10

Turnarounds

Turnarounds are critical for the character designer. It is important to understand the shape that you are turning and have a general understanding of human anatomy. Be sure to look at plane changes and perspective changes within each shape. Let's look at a human and see what you need to be aware of as you turn your character.

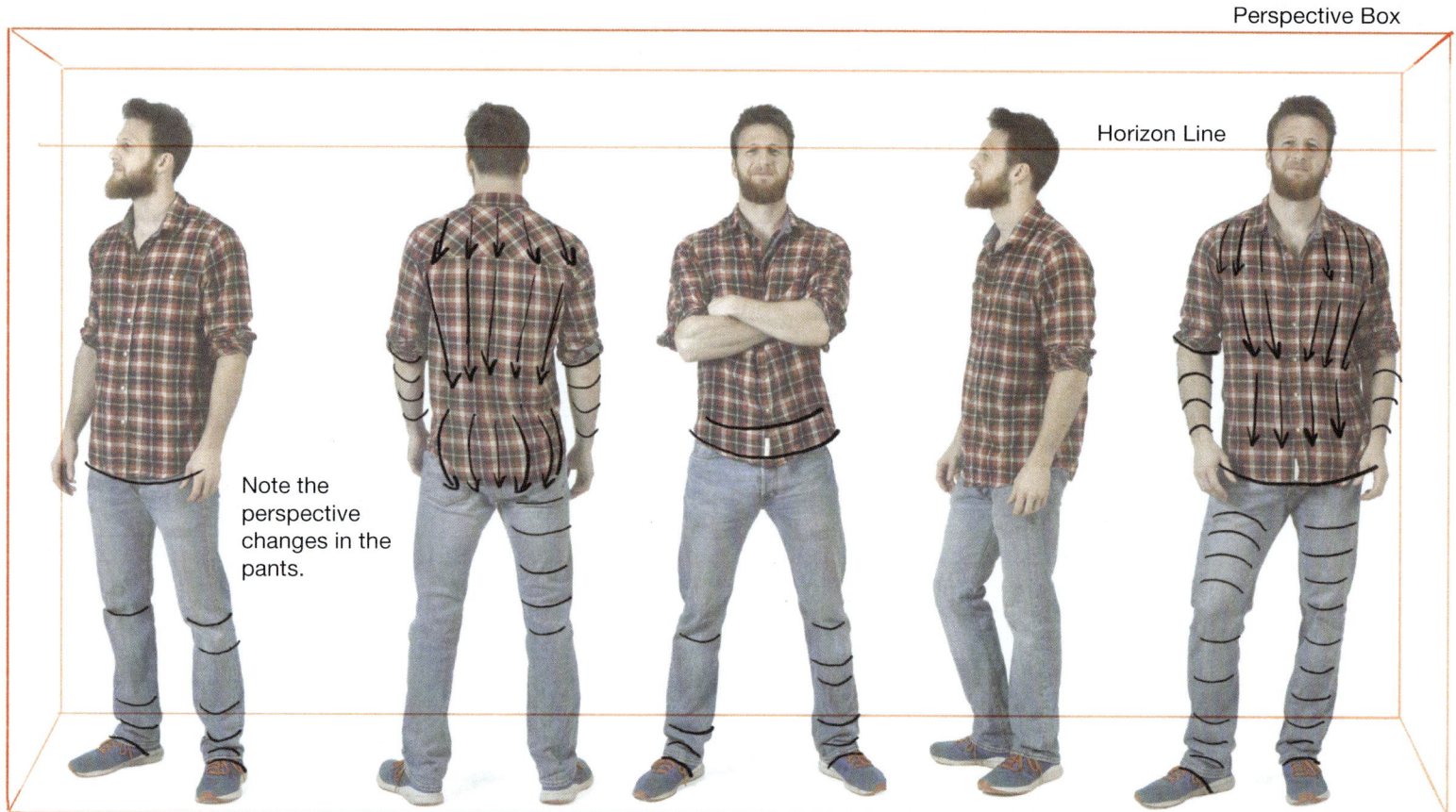

Perspective Box

Horizon Line

Note the perspective changes in the pants.

Take note of the plane changes in the back.

Note that the feet are facing downwards, NOT straight into the camera.

Pay attention to the direction of the limbs and shapes pants, shorts, skirts, wrinkles, stripes, etc. – as that will determine how you draw the perspectives on your clothing.

FIGURE 10.2
(REFERENCE: ADOBESTOCK_415845862)

In 2D turnarounds, think as if you were taking a photo of your pal and turning that pose of your pal. From your eye-line, THAT is the horizon line, and as you look downward toward the feet, you will see that the feet point in a slight downward fashion. It is this perspective that we see in most wide shots on film and TV shows.

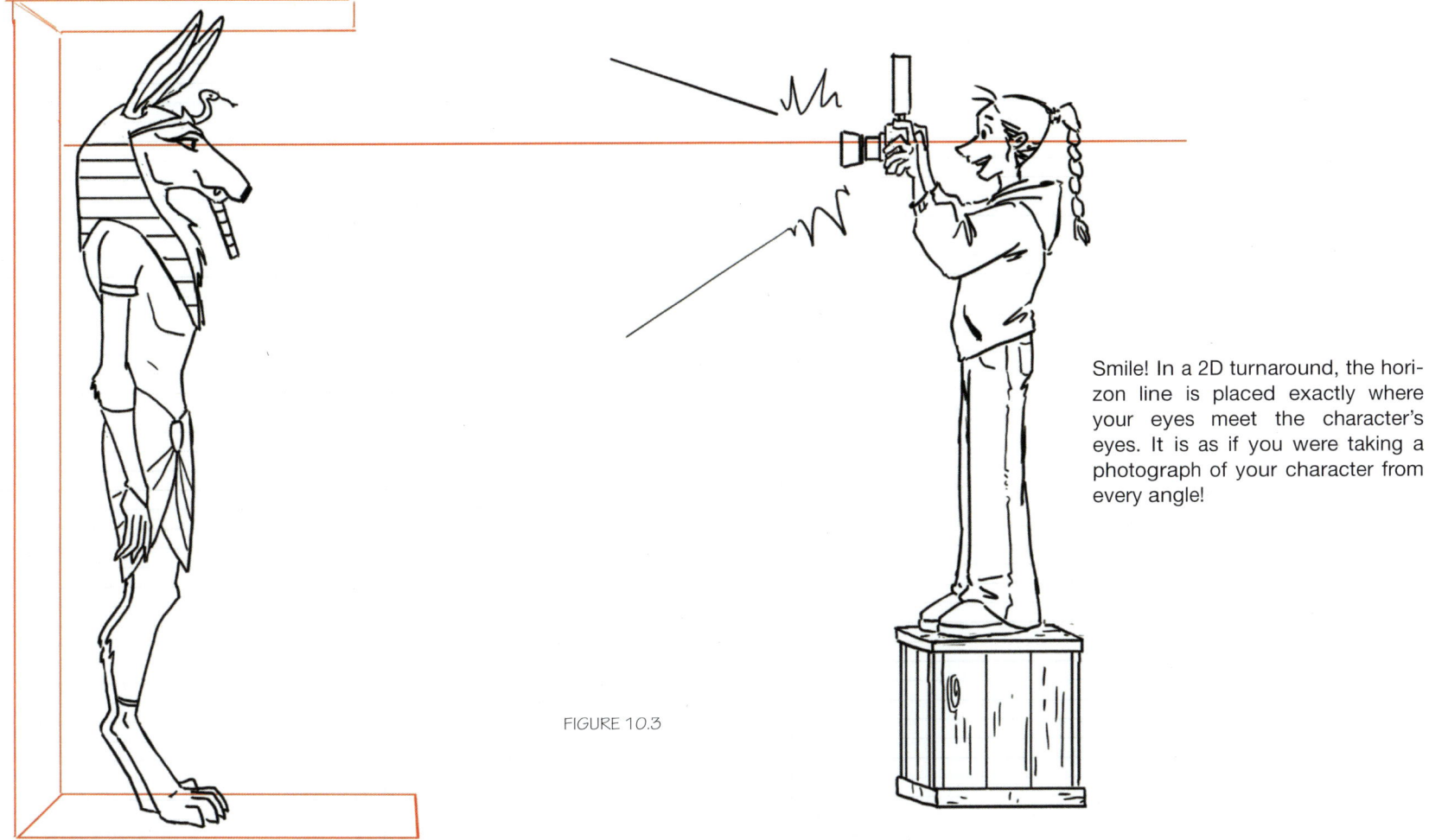

Smile! In a 2D turnaround, the horizon line is placed exactly where your eyes meet the character's eyes. It is as if you were taking a photograph of your character from every angle!

FIGURE 10.3

There is a big difference between a 2D turnaround and a 3D turnaround and that is the PERSPECTIVE.

In a 2D turnaround, the character is drawn in a ONE POINT PERSPECTIVE. Typically, the character is standing upright robot pose, arms down. When you turn the character, consider that the shapes on all aspects of the character will reflect the one-point perspective.

In a 3D turnaround, there is NO perspective. Every aspect of the character, from the clothes to the shoes to the head is FLAT. This is to help 3D modelers build the character accurately.

3D

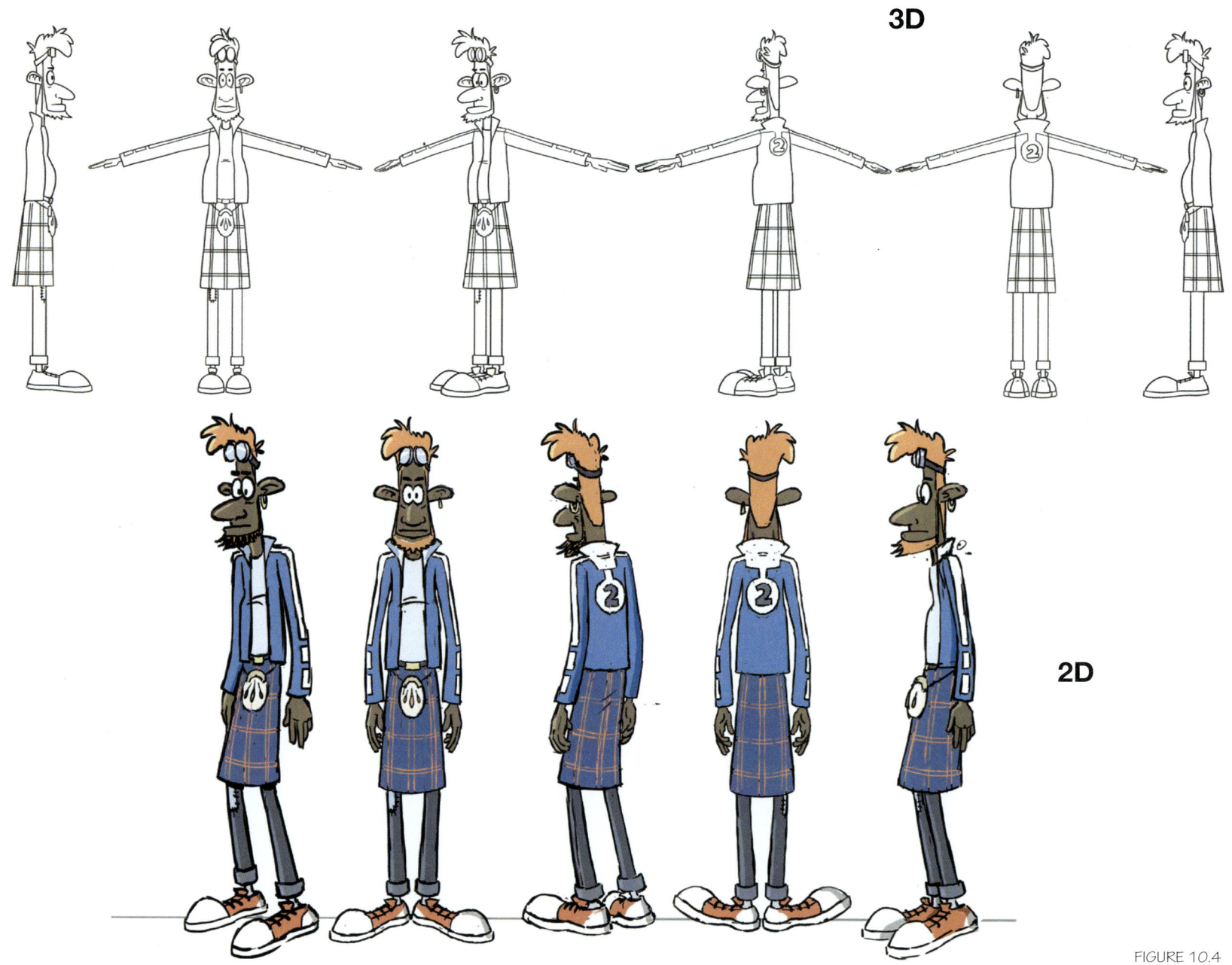

2D

FIGURE 10.4

Here's an example of a 2D Turnaround.

FRONT VIEW

Horizon Line

When drawing turn-arounds, start the pose in a stiff robot pose, arms down.

Take advantage of the tools your computer gives you. If your programs have a symmetry tool as well as a grid tool, then use it! Let your tools work for you and help you get the job done faster and with more accuracy.

It's generally best to start your turnarounds with either a clean front or 3/4 frontal pose. As you draw the character, make sure this character sits accurately in a perspective, with the horizon line at the eye line.

Perspective Box

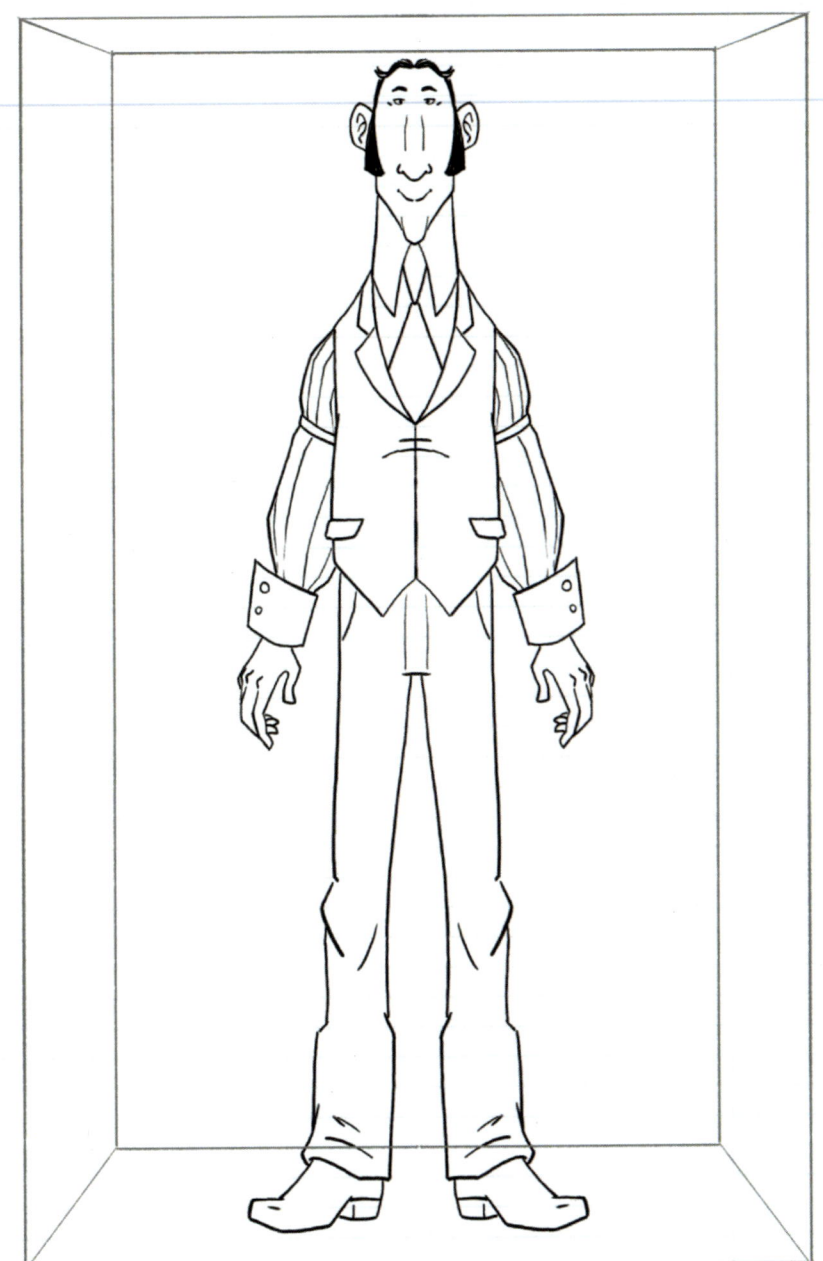

FIGURE 10.5

Draw Space - Draw your ideas and sketches here!

REAR VIEW

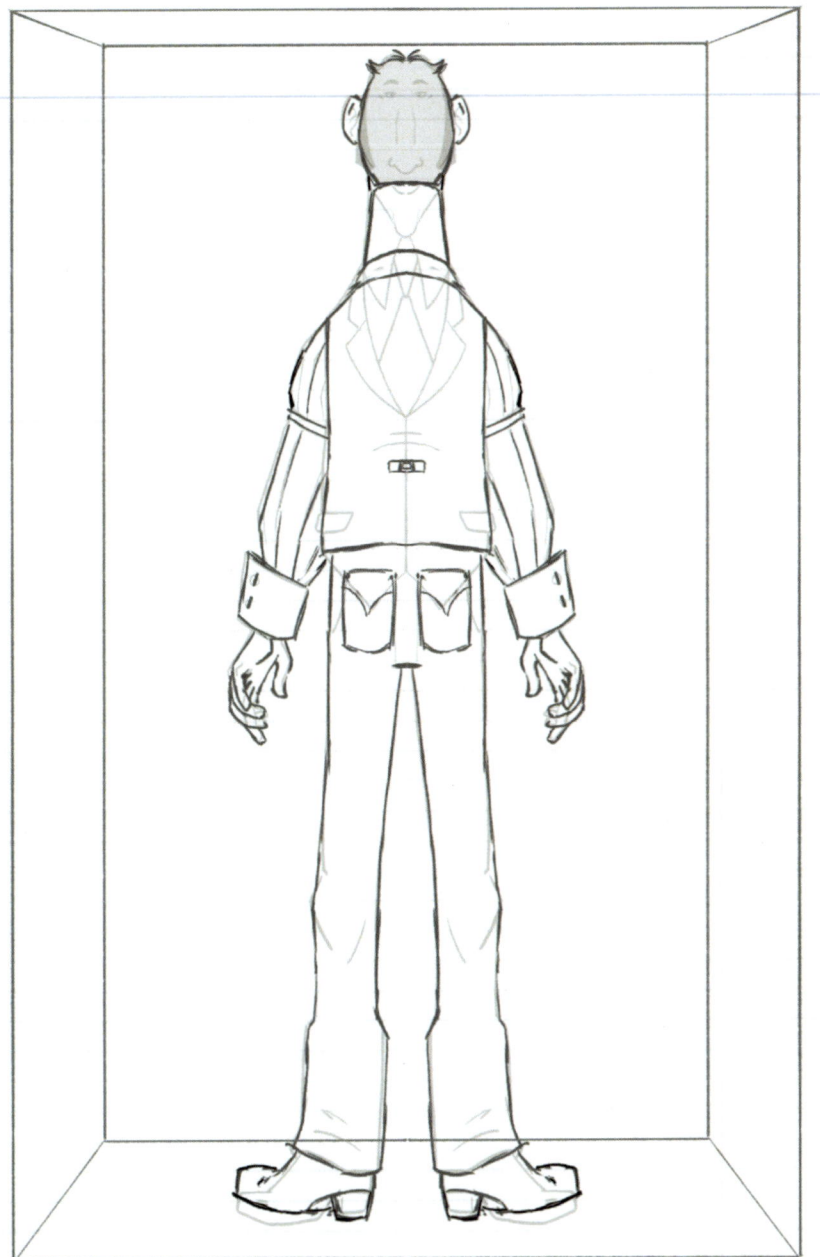

Horizon Line

When drawing the full rear, you can mostly trace from the frontal pose, by putting your rear pose directly on top of the frontal pose. There are some elements that you will have to resolve, such as the details of the rear of the jacket, pants, hands, etc.

Perspective Box

Note the feet point slightly upward as they are placed on this perspective plane.

FIGURE 10.6

Draw Space - Draw your ideas and sketches here!

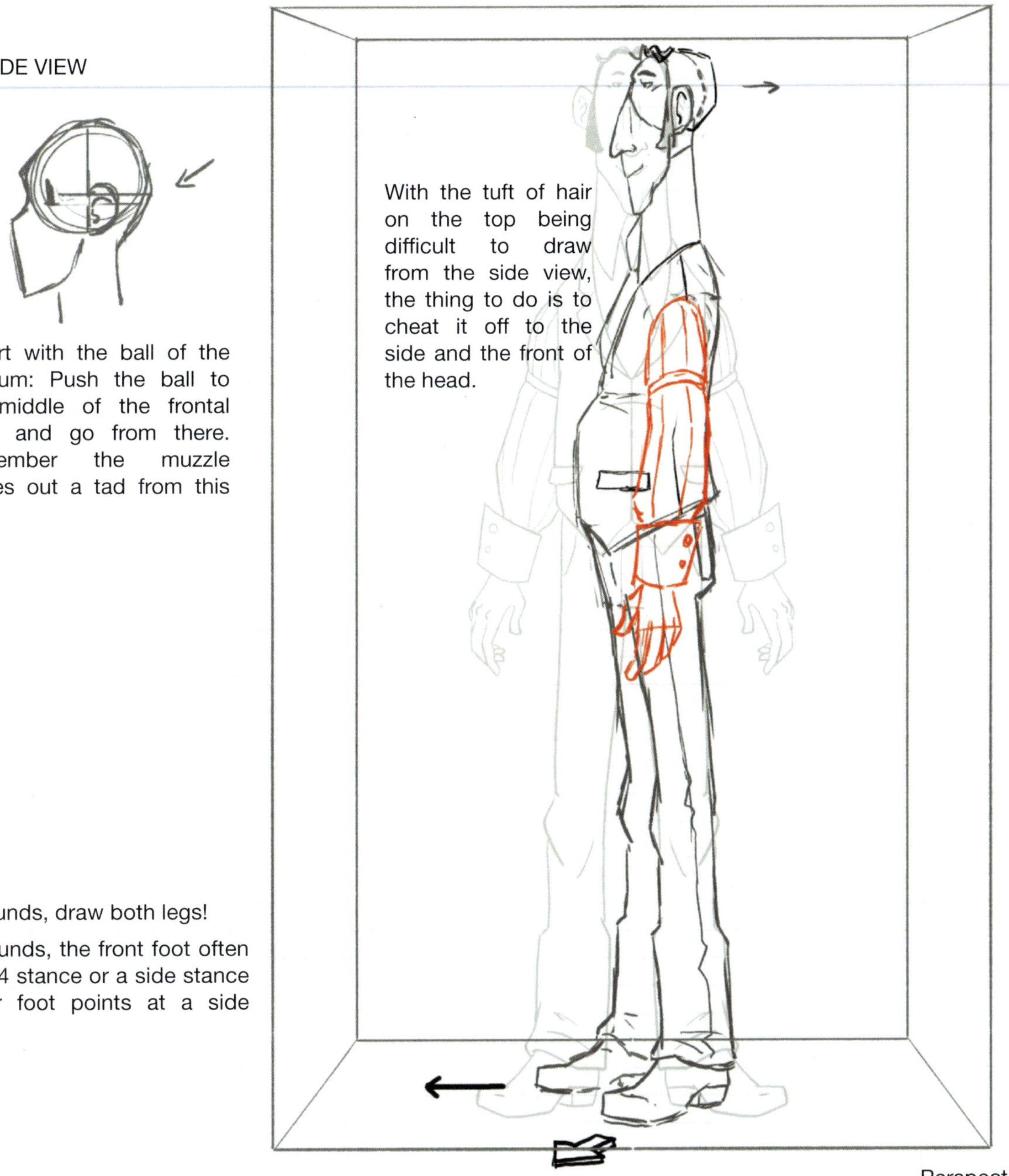

SIDE VIEW

I start with the ball of the cranium: Push the ball to the middle of the frontal pose and go from there. Remember the muzzle moves out a tad from this ball.

With the tuft of hair on the top being difficult to draw from the side view, the thing to do is to cheat it off to the side and the front of the head.

Horizon Line

It's best to put the arm on a separate layer.

When you are drawing the side view, you have to read the shapes in the first drawing and discover the shapes within the drawing. For example, the belly protrudes in the front drawing, so you will need to draw the belly protruding from the front side. The back follows the spine more closely.

In 2D turnarounds, draw both legs!

In 2D turnarounds, the front foot often points at a 3/4 stance or a side stance and the rear foot points at a side stance.

FIGURE 10.7

Perspective Box

Draw Space - Draw your ideas and sketches here!

3/4 FRONT VIEW

Horizon Line

When drawing the 3/4 front, draw ON TOP of the original drawing. That way, you can check the volumes and match lengths of every section of the body.

Shift the drawing to make sure the volumes in the torso and legs match and when you're happy with it, shift the sketch next to the original drawing and adjust anything to make sure the drawing looks appealing.

Perspective Box

Keep in mind, that the arms and legs that are CLOSEST are going to be slightly LONGER than the arms and legs that are the farthest away!

FIGURE 10.8

Draw Space - Draw your ideas and sketches here!

3/4 REAR VIEW

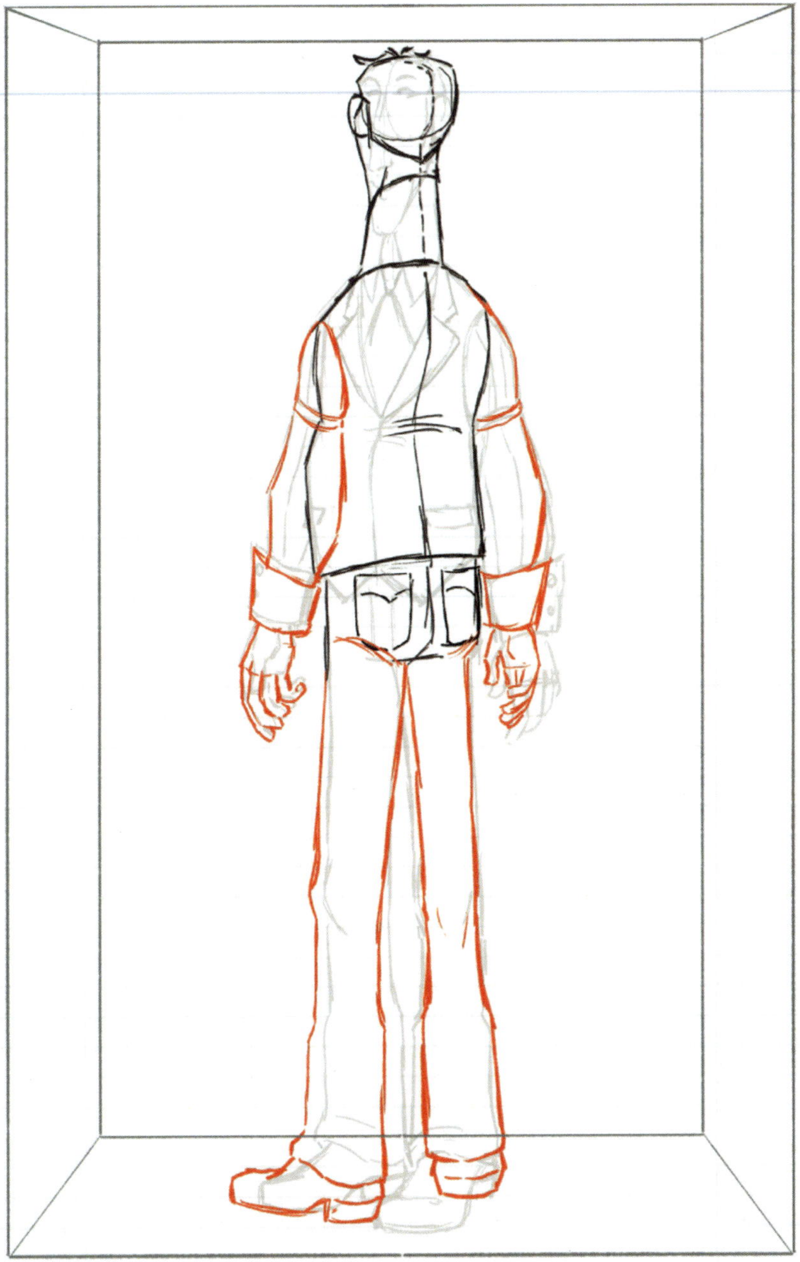

Horizon Line

Add some volume at the back of the head; otherwise, the head will look flat.

When doing the side view on semi-realistic characters, the ear is now in FRONT, rather than on the back of the head. Remember that the jaw connects to the ear!

When doing the 3/4 rear, there are some sections where you can 'trace', such as the head, the neck and the torso.

But there are sections that need to be drawn individually, in particular, the arms, hands, and legs.

Perspective Box

FIGURE 10.9

Draw Space - Draw your ideas and sketches here!

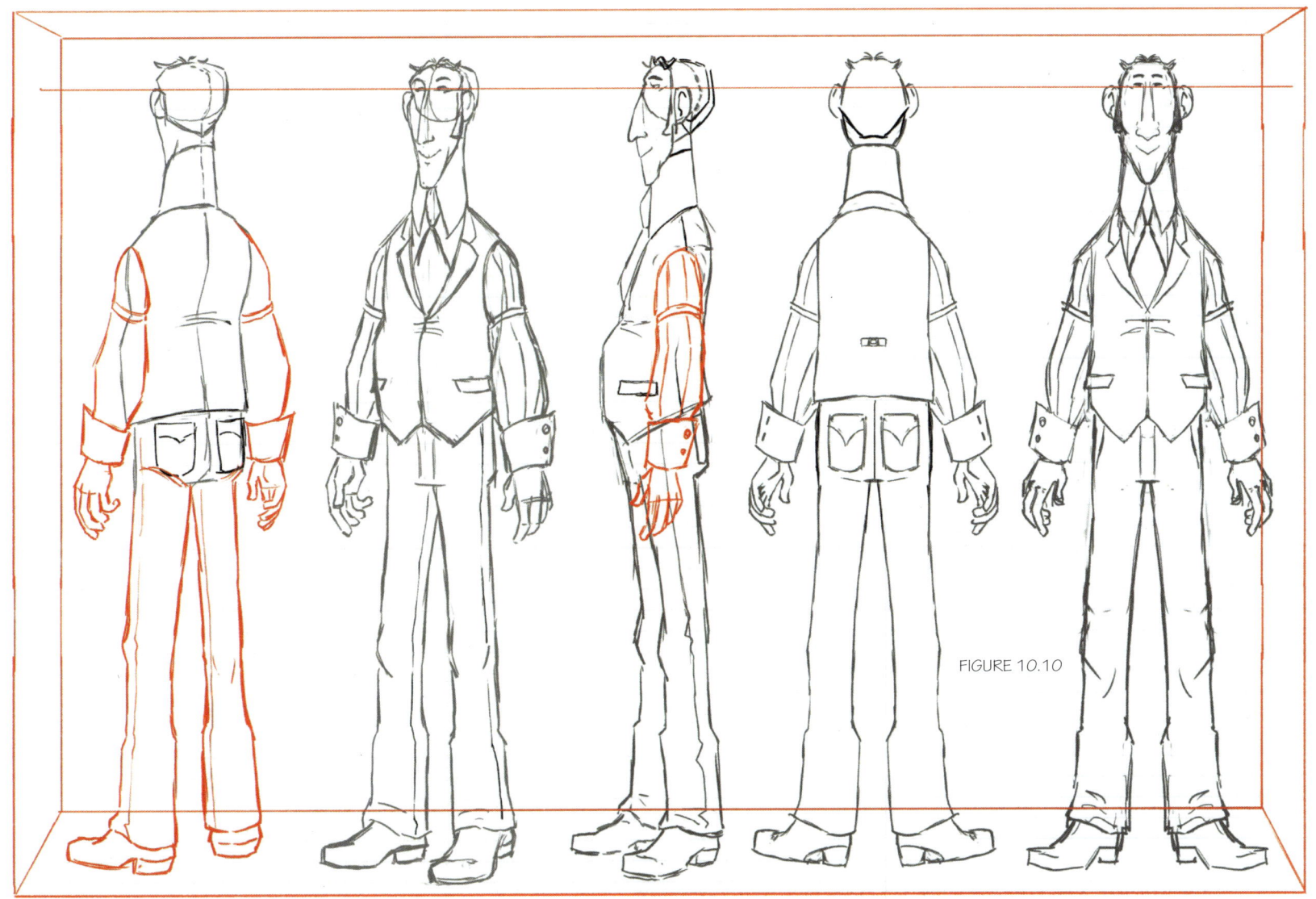

FIGURE 10.10

Once you have completed your turns, you can put all of them in a row and adjust and fix everything that seems off, so every single pose looks appealing, which is the goal for drawing solid turnarounds.

Draw Space - Draw your ideas and sketches here!

In the final turns, you can clean it up. Even in the clean up phase, you can find and fix any errors when you line up all your character side by side.

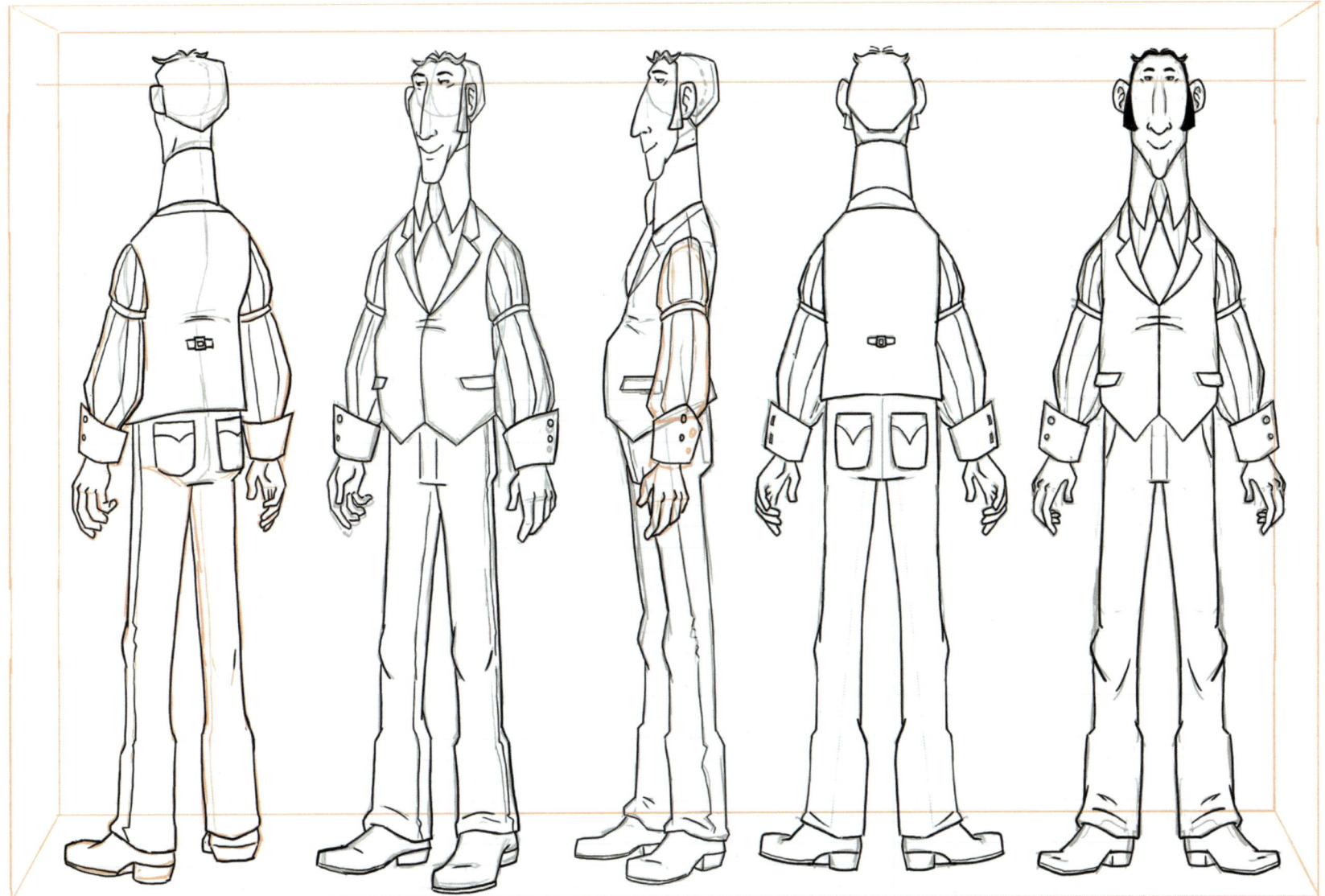

FIGURE 10.11

When you start doing your turnarounds, draw the FIRST angle nice and clean, so you can provide yourself and/or your team precise and accurate information for the rest of the turns.

Character designs handed to the turnaround designer are done in a ¾ or full frontal perspective. The horizon line is typically at the eyes so as you go down the body, your feet should point slightly downward, which is indicative of a 2D turnaround. Again, in a 3D turnaround, there is NO perspective so everything is flatly drawn, which is useful for 3D sculpting.

When I start turnarounds, I make sure to put my characters in a PERSPECTIVE BOX. Everything, from the limbs, hats, skirt, socks, collar, etc., will follow the perspective box and the perspective tube.

Front View

Horizon Line

FIGURE 10.12

Perspective Box

Perspective Tube

The perspective tube refers to perspectives on items such as skirts, socks, cuffs, hats, and shoes: How they angle on the figure should follow the perspective you have dictated for your character.

Draw Space - Draw your ideas and sketches here!

Rear View

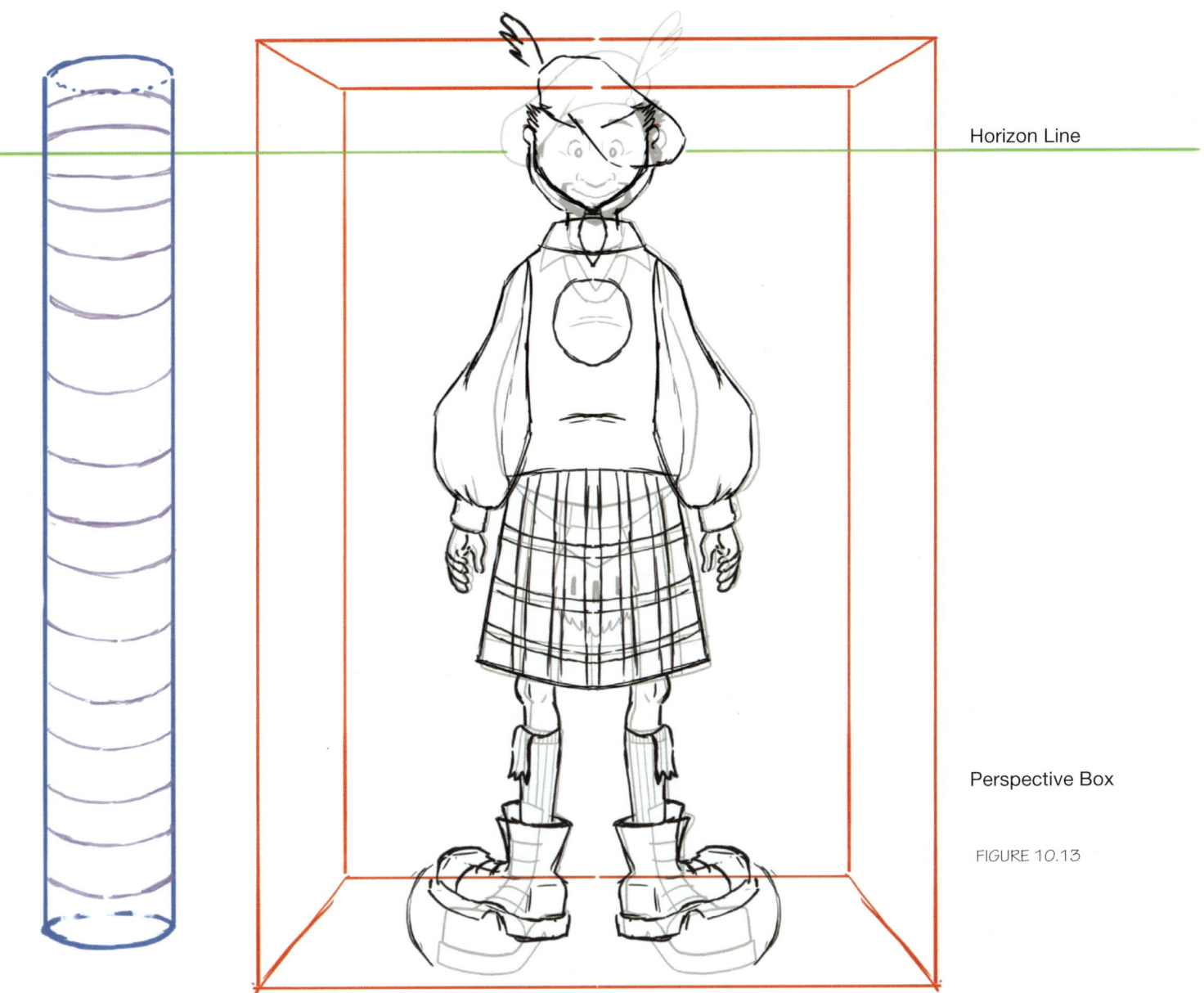

Horizon Line

Perspective Box

FIGURE 10.13

Draw Space - Draw your ideas and sketches here!

Side View

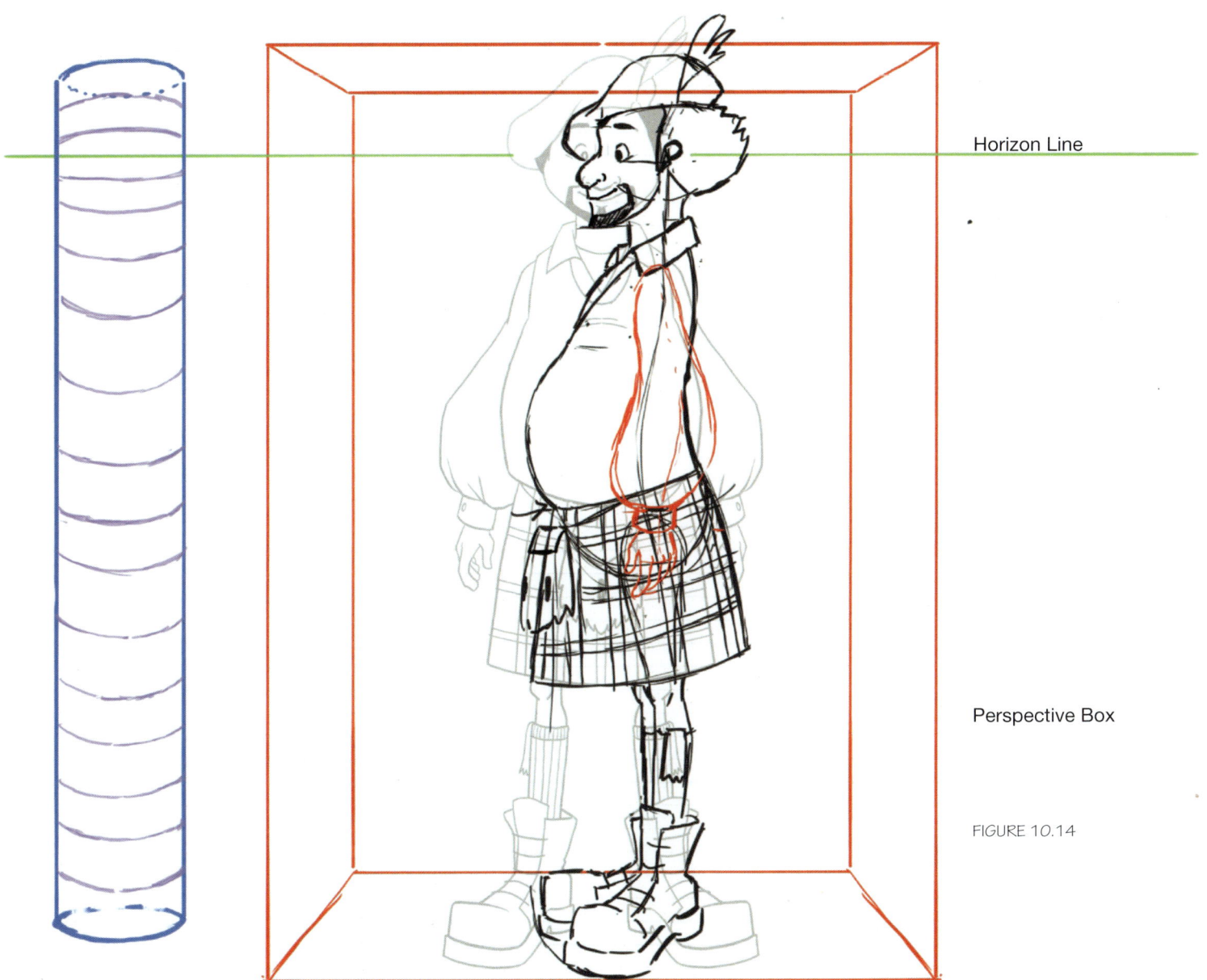

Horizon Line

Perspective Box

FIGURE 10.14

Draw Space - Draw your ideas and sketches here!

¾ Front

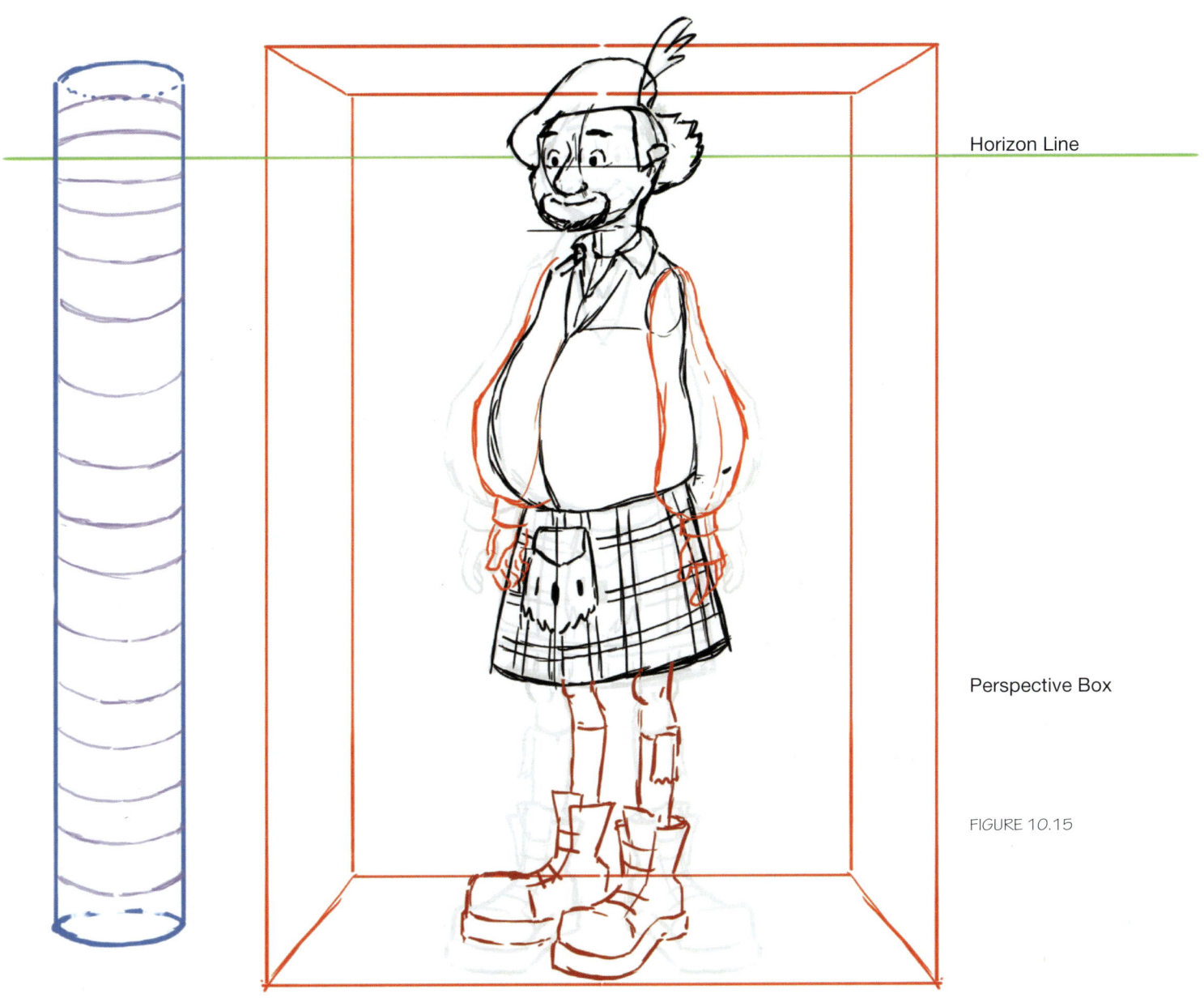

Horizon Line

Perspective Box

FIGURE 10.15

Draw Space - Draw your ideas and sketches here!

¾ Rear

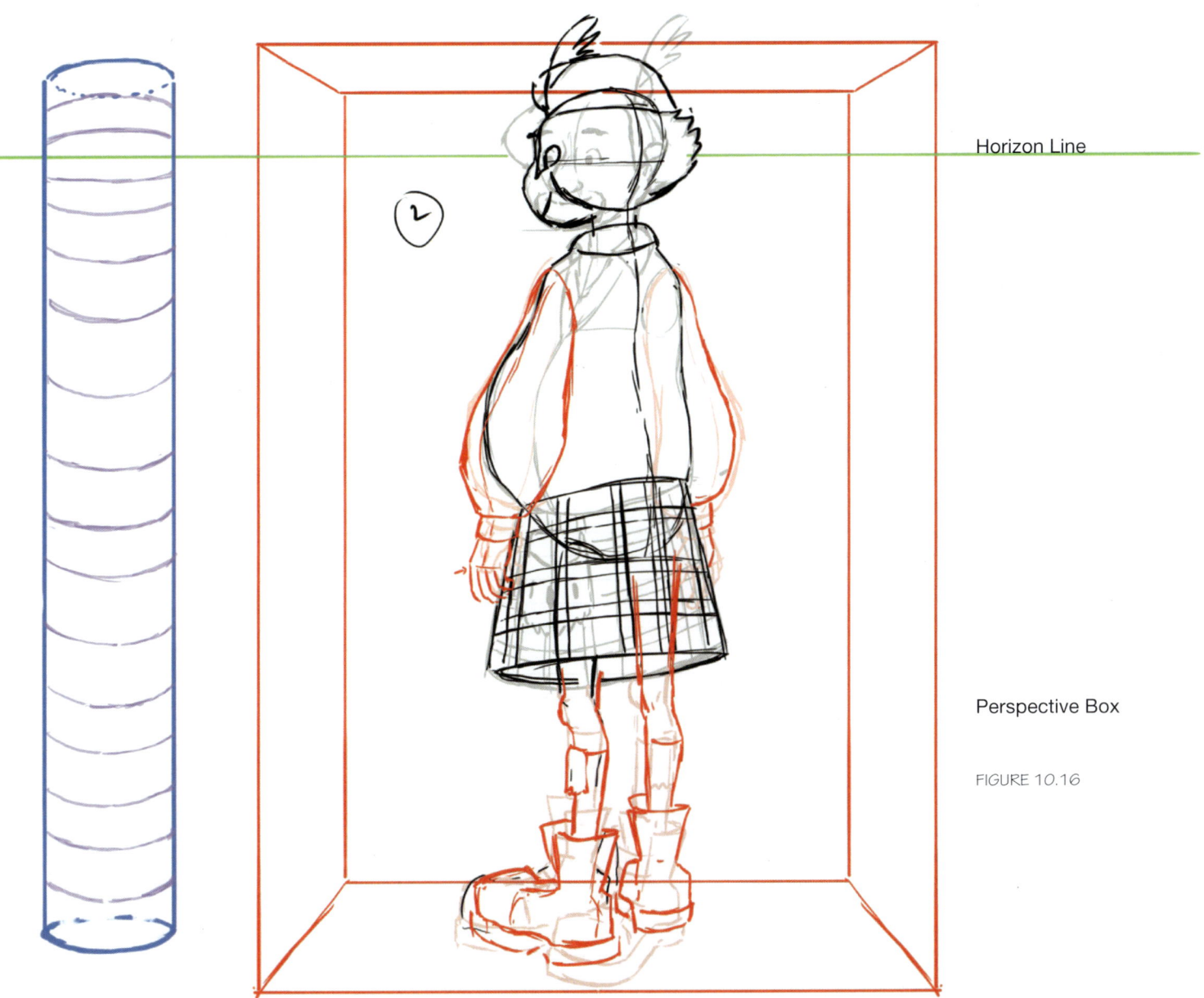

Horizon Line

Perspective Box

FIGURE 10.16

Draw Space - Draw your ideas and sketches here!

After turning them, line up the characters. You can fix a lot of errors in this stage!

FIGURE 10.17

Draw Space - Draw your ideas and sketches here!

Final Cleanup

FIGURE 10.18

Draw Space - Draw your ideas and sketches here!

Some designs are of the limited animation variety, so turnarounds can be limited to just three sides: ¾ front, ¾ rear, and side.

Anytime you have a character with a lot of hair or a cape or anything that covers other parts of the body, you will need to draw the character underneath and make an extra layer for the cape or hair.

This design comes from a thumbnail.

FIGURE 10.19

Draw Space - Draw your ideas and sketches here!

Note this turnaround of an anthropomorphic character: When a character has a slouch, you will have to show the neck on the other views. The character is hunched, so be sure to determine the shape of the torso on the side views and 3/4 views.

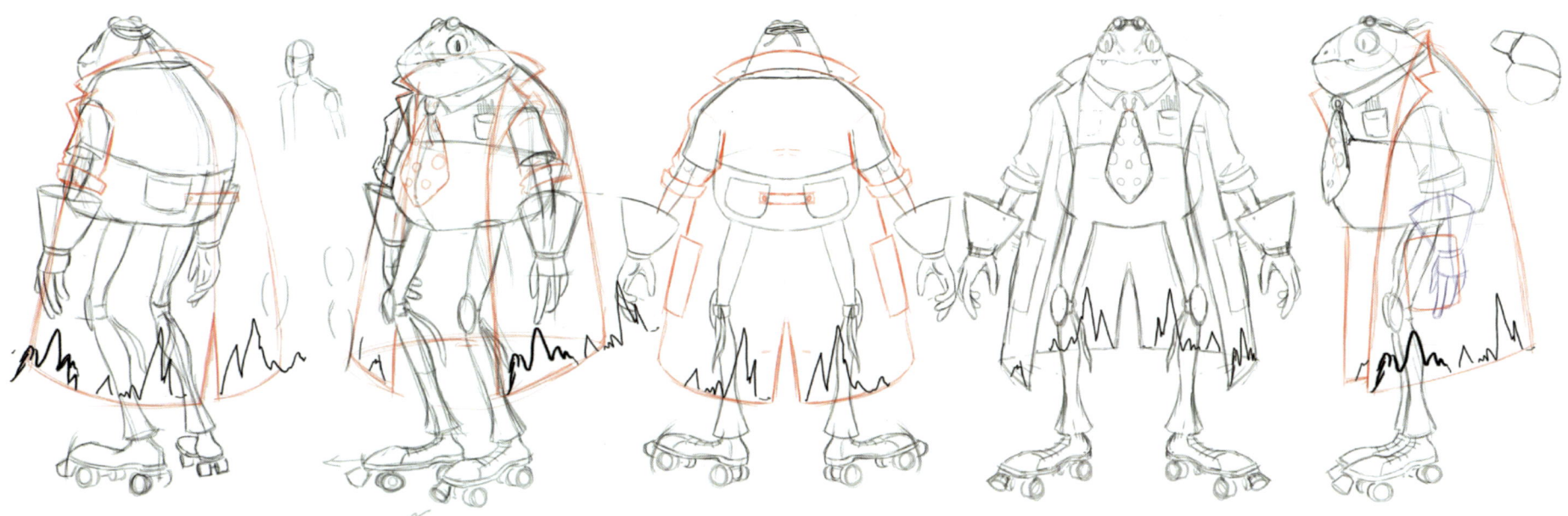

FIGURE 10.20

Draw Space - Draw your ideas and sketches here!

In the cleanup phase, you can add further details, such as tears on the jacket, pockets, and things: Turnarounds can also entail full color on all your characters, but exactness is key and that's where your knowledge of shapes is critical. Take your time making sure all angles of your standing character are appealing on all sides, so you may have to cheat certain aspects of your character, such as the tail, hair and nose (look closely at the Mickey Mouse, Goofy or Daffy Duck turnarounds, in particular, the nose and beak!) – and that's okay as long as the character looks good at that angle!

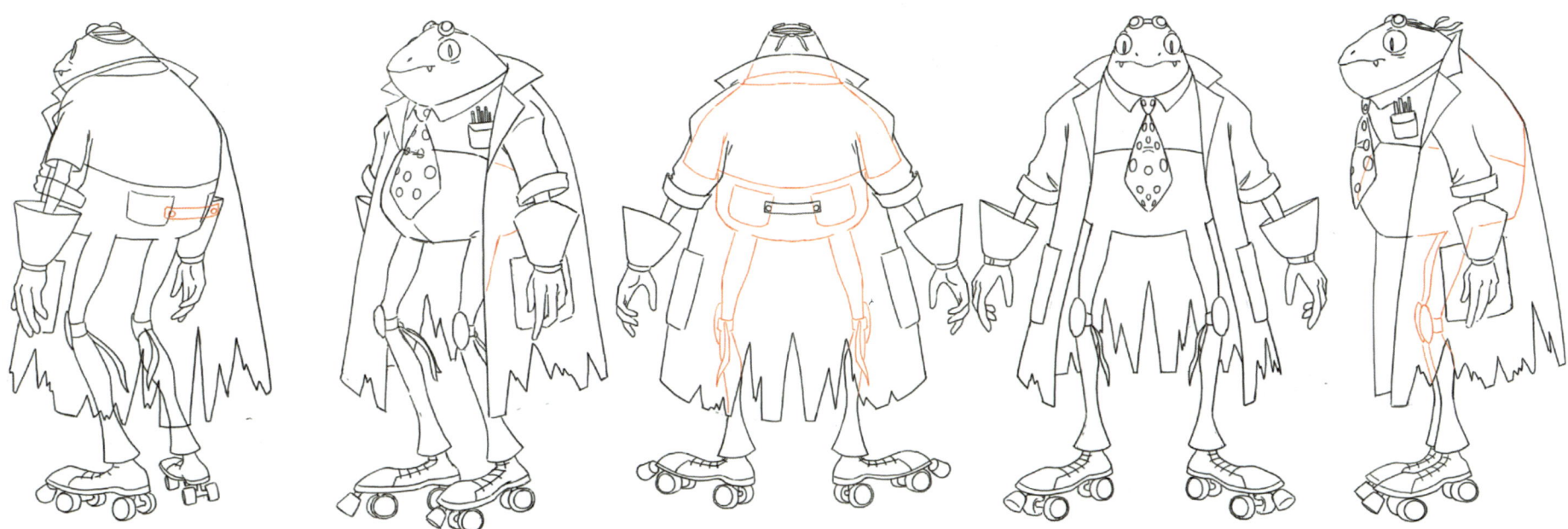

FIGURE 10.21

Final Stuff...

What you need to do – as you draw – is to know and understand the shapes of every aspect of your character design, in whatever style you have chosen. Great design entails a variation of shape, size, and silhouette as well as solidity and fluidity. Once you have that understanding, turning your characters will be easy!

Just know that every line you put down has a specific purpose to your character's design, that it fills a void, a volume, or an action. If you understand what line you're putting down has structure inside it, you can move it in any direction and push that design as far as you can go.

The good thing to think about is that your character or characters are the subjects the audience will see on film, and it is your responsibility to make these characters fun to look at, admire, loathe, fall in love with! Go as far as you can go with your ideas and push yourself to the limits and MAKE. GREAT. ART.

FIGURE 11.1

DOI: 10.1201/9781003599005-11

Index